MW01147415

BAD THEOLOGY KILLS

Undoing Toxic Beliefs & Reclaiming Your Spiritual Authority.

Kevin Miguel Garcia

Foreward by Mike McHargue

Copyright © 2020 Kevin Garcia

All rights reserved. With the exception of limited quotations
attributed to the author for the use of academia, research, review,
or social media, no part of this book may be reproduced without
express permission from the author.

ISBN: 9781656651808

To the younger me:

You once asked a question in your journal.
"Isn't it enough to simply love?"

You were right. You were right the whole time.

CONTENTS

BEFORE WE BEGIN (AGAIN)
A QUICK WORD ON THE SECOND EDITION OF
BAD THEOLOGY KILLS

There was a part of me that was really nervous about doing this whole thing myself. I was afraid I'd miss something in the editing, that it wasn't going to go anywhere, that people wouldn't read it, and that this would be among the litany of failed book attempts I made before. However, I'm delighted to now find myself almost a year later having had my book reach thousands of people across the planet. The message of Bad Theology Kills has touched so many folks, and it's beginning to be an easy, blunt, and effective explanation as to why so many of us move away from harmful institutions.

The great thing about self-publishing this book was that I got to keep all the rights to it, give it away as much as I want. It also means I have to own the mistakes that were in it. And by mistakes, I mean proofreading and just a few passages that didn't read well. But what I'll hang my hat on is the content.

As I read thru this book again with a fine-tooth comb, in addition to fixing the errors, I found that there was a bit more I needed and wanted to say in many places. I wrote this book at the end of 2019, before 2020 and the pandemic and the uprising in support for the Black Lives Matter movement. I wrote it and put it out in somewhat of a hurry, and there was still so much I didn't get into. But the best part about all of it is that I own this book. Being self-published means I get to add or edit the text, and make it the best possible thing it could be. And that's exactly what I wanted to do here in this second edition.

What you'll find in this book is just a little more expansion of what was in the original manuscript, with a focus on how everything intersects, interlocks, and overlaps with everything else. There's more of an emphasis on racial dynamics, as well as how Christianity and colonialism are bed fellows. And you'll also find that silly mistakes and errors will be gone. (And when you find them, just circle them, laugh a little bit, and say, "of course.")

Thank you to everyone for supporting this work, for sharing this message far and wide. Keep going. The Light is already here. We just need to keep shining.

-Kevin Garcia,
Atlanta, GA, December 2020

FOREWARD

I believe the title of this book is right: "*Bad Theology Kills.*" The book isn't called "*Bad Theology is Troublesome,*" or "*Bad Theology is Difficult,*" because the stakes of toxic Christianity are life and death for millions of people. I have lost friends to bad theology, both in broken relationships because of my actions, and to death by suicide.

Could I ask you to pause for a moment? I'd like you to become aware that you are reading a book right now, that you are in a physical space somewhere, and that you aren't a disembodied observer. With that awareness, take a moment to read the following statements and notice what happens with your feelings:

Bad Theology Kills.

Toxic Christianity.

I would imagine that for some of you, there may be a sense of relief as you read those words. *Finally,* you may think, *someone is saying this out loud at last.* To you, I say, "Welcome, my friend Kevin is about to speak a truth you have been dying to hear."

Others may feel a sense of anxiousness or defensiveness. You may think, *what have I gotten myself into,* or, *is this book safe.* You may even think, *is this book biblical.* Perhaps there is something else underneath all these thoughts. Years ago, as I first started to wrestle with the impact of my theology on the lives of other people, all these questions sat on another, foundational question: *am I a good person.*

My friend Kevin is queer. That may lead you to believe that this is a book about sexuality, gender identity, and faith. And, yes, certainly those themes are explored deeply in this book. But, to limit the scope of bad theology and its impact on LGBTQ issues is to miss the full arc of what Kevin does in the following pages.

You see, this is a book about shame. And loss.

This is a book about identity. And community.

But, most of all, this is a book about God. And love. And how God and love are the same thing--and the scandalous, beautiful implications of that fundamental notion.

Kevin is right. Bad Theology Kills. But, in this book, Kevin shows us something else, something so exciting to me that I could not put the book down once I started reading it.

Good Theology Brings Life;
and,
Christianity doesn't have to be toxic.

Thank you for showing us the way, Kevin. I know these insights came to you at a high cost.

–Mike McHargue
  Los Angeles, CA

BEFORE WE BEGIN:
AN INTRODUCTION (I GUESS)

Before we begin, I want you to hear something that maybe you haven't heard before. Well, maybe you have, but I *really* want you to get this.

You've already been forgiven.

That's the scandal of this whole thing. Our entire lives, we've been convinced that everything has a price. We were taught that our salvation was bought at a price. We learned our sins and transgressions were paid for by a brown not very well-liked prophet who was murdered by an empire. Because of this, you and I (and every other human who is alive since the time of Jesus) apparently have a choice: to either devote ourselves to a very particular way of being in the world, so that we may live into our identities in Christ and be saved from eternal conscious torment, or not.

But, again, this isn't true.

It is impossible to live outside of God. It is impossible to not have the Christ in you. It is impossible to be without the Holy Spirit. While it is possible to live out of alignment, to simply not hear the voice of God speaking to you through the beautiful temple that is your body, you are never separate from Love.

And you might say, "Well, that sounds like heresy." According to who?
You?
Your pastor?
The Bible you claim to take so literally?

I'd argue that the majority of Christian practices, especially in

1

Evangelicalism that I grew up in, are heretical. Furthermore, I'd say they are, in fact, anti-Christ.

In a desire to be pro-life, evangelicals and conservatives still deny protection to the living. They do nothing to protect the most vulnerable people in your communities through something as simple as common-sense gun reform. Thus, I contest that the religious right has lost all authority to dictate morality.

Let me ask you something: why do you believe what you do? This is not a question to be combative, although the ego would like to think that any probing question is an attack. It's not. I'm genuinely curious why you believe what you do. What got you here? What voices have you been listening to?

The apostle Peter tells us to always be "ready to make a defense to anyone who asks you to give an account for the hope that is in you, yet with gentleness and reverence..."[1] Notice he's not asking you to defend Jesus. He's not asking you to protect God or even the Church or the holy scriptures. Peter wants you to know why you believe what you do and to be ready to share that reason.

What I find most often when speaking with either conservative Christians or folks who end up on the outside of the Church for one reason or another, I find the same thing to be true.

We don't know why we believe what we do.

We've spent our whole lives wrapped up in a system that provided us our answers. Now that we find ourselves on the far side of deconstruction of our toxic faith systems, we don't know what to do. The Church raised us to be codependent on it, continuously existing in a state of crisis, attempting to appease an angry god, and by extension, please the men who served him. And now that we are out of survival mode, we barely know how to function in the real world.

Or maybe you are someone who spent your whole life devoid of a spiritual system, and you don't carry the religious baggage. Yet, still, you recognize there's a disconnect between how you were told the world worked, how it actually works, and how you fit into the whole thing.

It's all boils down to one thing: *bad theology*. It's shitty ways of talking about,

---

[1] 1 Peter 3:15 NASB

2

thinking about, interacting with what we call God. It's scripts and behavioral patterns that continue to play themselves out over and over again. It's an oppressive system, continually forcing you to compete, to shine brighter than the person next to you, to be more woke than the next asshole on Twitter, to be sexier than your Tinder profile when you show up in real life, to practice gratitude and forget your pain because joy is evidence of God's presence and blessing, be perfect therefore as your father in heaven is perfect, pray more, live with intention and also work from your rest... holy shit.

How exhausting.

We are all out here trying to work for our forgiveness. We're all out here trying to make ourselves worthy of Love. And yet, even by the most conservative standards of Christian faith, there is nothing that we can do to make God love us less or love us more. If that's true, why the fuck are we all so worried about trying to keep God happy?

Ain't you tired, babe?
Ain't you tired of always questioning because you always need to know?
Ain't you tired of having to defend yourself to everyone?
Ain't you tired of feeling like you are always a step behind?
Ain't you tired of needing to measure up to a standard that is too high?
Ain't you tired, babe?

Well, if I may, I'd like to remind you of the first thing we started from: you're already forgiven.

You are a child of God, and you are a temple of God. God is present in the atoms that make up the cells that make up the blood and guts and systems of your body. God is as close as the electrical currents that are firing at rapid speed in the grey matter that is your brain, helping you decipher these symbols into words and sentences, rendering them into phrases and meaning.

God is in all of it. God *is* all of it.

So, if we are already forgiven, why is it that we always feel so bad about ourselves? Why do we feel so disconnected from everything and everyone, even our own bodies?

Because we do not believe it. We don't understand the gospel that God is

Love, that the Kin'dom[2] is at hand, that all who call upon the name of the Lord shall be saved. What would it be like to believe that? Like for real. What would it be like to think that at the core of who you are, the very essence of your being, was untouchable but endlessly knowable, incorruptible, and good? That there was goodness and connection and light, instead of the corrupted and distorted desire for things that would bring us or others harm?

It's because we live in a world that has been marred by the human capacity to fuck shit up. (Some folks call that sin.) We evolved in a violent world. That violence shaped our species. It separated us from God. It still separates people from God. It is the job of God's people to end that violence, to mend that separation, and to wake people to the reality that the division was only an illusion.

Be it gun violence, laws that infringe on a woman's body, policies that actively police people's gender presentation and identity, a police state that kills black folks without recompense, attitudes and teachings that make queer folks kill themselves, cultural constructs that define how we relate to our bodies, the shame we feel around sex and desire, bad theology that props up oppressive systems or governments that claim to be representatives of a religion of radical love and justice but in truth are perpetuating more violence— It is the call of God's people to break the cycle.

I remember back in my Pentecostal days; we'd often talk about generational curses. And those are absolutely real. A generational curse is a pattern of attitudes, behaviors, and actions that are passed onto the next generation. It builds up a callus over infected wounds of our hearts until the pain is so great a generation wakes up, uncovers the pain, and begins the hard work of healing.

Dearest siblings, I want to declare to you today that the curse stops with us.

I believe we are the ones to end it. We will be the ones to wake up. We will be the ones to marry an expansive, robust, authentic spiritual connection

---

[2] "Kin'dom" of God is term developed in liberation and womanist theologies as an alternative to "Kingdom" of God, as God's kingdom is nothing like the kingdoms of this world. It is imagined to be one where hierarchy is done away with, and thus a dominion and community of kin. My use of this term is a nod to that, and personally I like it better. Read more from *Kin-dom of God: A Mujerista Proposal* by Ada Maria Isasi-Diaz.

with practical, organized acts of radical love. We will be the Church, but not in the sense that we will have buildings or denominations, but in the sense that we will live into our role as the manifest presence of Love on the earth.

Bad theology is killing us. It's time to name it and exorcise it from our bodies and our communities. Bad theology is killing my queer family through gun violence and economic barriers and laws. Bad theology is killing my friends of color through systemic discrimination and racially based injustice. Bad theology is killing me, you, your friends, your family, your churches, your community, your country, your world.

Bad theology is killing our imagination.

Our imagination, the seat of our prophetic sight, has been constricted for too long. That is why so many of us cannot fulfill the words Peter calls us to do, to give a reason for the hope we have because hope is in short supply. And when hope is in short supply, faith is in short supply. If our faith is in short supply, we will never find the love we so desperately need to resurrect our hearts and souls, nor the hearts and souls of our world and faith traditions.

So, let us imagine what an antidote to toxic Christianity and toxic religion all around could be. Your cynicism will tell you that it's not possible. Your data-driven, social media soaked mind may say that it's a fool's errand to try and change the world, but I'm not concerned with the whole world. I'm first and foremost concerned with myself. This concern is not selfish, as I was raised to believe. The concern for the wellbeing of my soul springs from my desire and purpose to love the world back to health, as God so loves the world and wants to see it survive and thrive. And so, it should be with you.

Can you imagine what it would be like? To have a faith where you weren't afraid? To speak to God without wondering if your prayers were being heard? To hold both your doubt and trust in the same hand, not needing to let go of either? What would it be like to release your fear of hell and the wrath of an angry God? What would it be like to love your neighbor wholeheartedly? What would it be like to love your children completely? What would it be like to forgive people who hurt you? Or, better still, what it would be like to love and forgive yourself without caveat or restrictions?

Pretty sure Jesus said something about that.

This book is as much an attempt at making sense of my own theology and to affirm at the same time that none of it matters if I do not hold on to the truth: *I am beloved*. This unshakable and unquestionable spiritual law is what led me here. It continues to lead me into more and more freedom.

Claiming that freedom was a painful process. Losing my faith community and people who I counted as my closest friends and wrecking my worldview for the sake of discovering something true was difficult. But I give thanks. These experiences stripped me of everything unnecessary; everything that was not the voice of God. By the time my faith fell like a house of cards, I had nothing left to lose.

And there is nothing more dangerous than someone with nothing to lose.

1
BUT I DON'T FEEL BAD...

I'm sitting on a mountain right now with my friends. People I met through the internet, and through struggle and grief and tears and work and a desire to see each other succeed, I've finally realized what Jesus was talking about when he asked who his family was. It's the ones around me, the ones who see me. Not the internet version of me (as much as I'd like to think there is no difference, there's always a slight performance and projection), the real me. I don't need any qualifiers. I don't need to feel self-conscious that I'm being judged. These people remind me of who I am, especially on the days when I feel like the worst version of myself. They see the David, where I only see a hunk of marble.

They remind me that I am:
Beloved
Whole
Needed
Wanted
Powerful
Imperfect
And good.

The actions I take speak to the kind of person I am. My attitude toward humanity dictates what I believe. It is not a matter of what I claim to value or what I say I believe. Faith without action is dead, is it not? So, wouldn't my actions speak to what I believe? Because we all know someone who says they love God and yet they are literally the *worst* kind of human. On the flip side, we see people who identify as Atheists do more good for people than the entire cast of the 700 Club ever could.

Dietrich Bonhoeffer said, in *The Cost of Discipleship,* that if one claims to believe in Christ but does not do what Christ commands, they don't honestly believe. But if one does the will of Christ, then that person believes. It is curious to me that even as I type these words, I wonder if I am a Christian.

Because if being a Christian means that I vote Republican and think abortion is almost as egregious a sin as being a practicing homosexual, then no, I'm not a Christian. If being a Christian means that I believe everyone should attend a church and give their money to their local congregation, or that they should be reading their Bible every day, then no, I'm not a Christian. If being a Christian means I have to take every word of the Bible as straight from the anthropomorphized lips of God Herself, then no, I am not a Christian. If being a Christian means I have to affirm a literal virgin birth, literal death *and* resurrection, or any literal tongues of fire, then no, I am not a Christian.

If I can be honest with you, I don't *care.* I wish I could care about that label anymore, but I just don't. And that is so freeing for me. Because now, I'm free to do the work of healing. I'm not working or looking for the approval of anyone to tell me if my connection to God is real or not. I know it's real. My experiences and my body has confirmed it over and over again. In fact, since I stopped trying to be a Christian, I've been more connected to God than I ever thought possible. Someone else's belief in the validity of my story does not affirm or negate the truth of my experiences.

...

When I was nine years old, I was at a Jesus camp in the backwoods of Tennessee. At the altar call, I said out loud that I wanted God to guide me, and that I wanted God to make His home in me, that I would be set free to love more. I felt, in that moment, an upwelling of joy and light so tangible that I laughed and cried and shouted because I was so aware of how much God loved me. I could feel the presence of the Holy, and it was as if it was always there, but something was covering it up. And for a brief moment, I knew I was in Love. Not in love, but in Love.

Let me explain.

To be in Love is to be so caught up in the reality of our communion with

God that we naturally flow in our purpose, bringing healing to everyone around us. It is our natural state. It is where we came from and to where we will return. When we can remember that we are included in Love, our lives become richer.

That was the first moment I knew God was real. It was the first moment I realized that what I was experiencing of God was different than the people around me. I felt joy and laughter, and also this just intense crying because of the visceral happiness that was manifesting in me. When I didn't calm down, I was told I needed to stop being so dramatic. But what was so dramatic of reveling in the Truth? The Truth that God loves me. It didn't make sense. Didn't they feel the same thing as me? Isn't this what Jesus talked about?

But I didn't know any better. They let me know in no uncertain terms that I didn't know anything, and if I wanted answers, I had to ask them. They were my elders and my leaders, and they'd been walking with Jesus a lot longer than me, so their advice should be followed. I learned at that moment that anything that came from within, anything my body was telling me, was probably wrong. The urge to dance, the urge to be too expressive, the urge to ask questions, I stopped all of that. I wanted to be a man of God, and a man of God looked like my uncle, my father and my youth pastor. I wanted to be a good Christian.

So, I learned what that meant and executed it well. I read my Bible devotionals every day in my quiet time. I prayed often and fervently. I served on the church's worship team. I kept my grades up, didn't have sex, drink or do drugs, or cuss. Because I did these things, I knew I was a good Christian. I belonged. I was praised for my behavior. I knew that because I did these things, God was pleased with me. Because my only desire was for the kingdom of God. It was all I would seek. And God would bless me because God desired to give good gifts to His children.

And then I noticed a boy for the first time.

Jesus Christ, no! The thought crept across my mind, and time seemed to be suspended. I didn't just notice that he was a boy, I noticed that his jawline was perfect, and his eyes were bright like a clear, noonday sky. I saw the way his legs fit in his skinny jeans and how the outline of his groin looked. My eyes traced the veins in his soft-looking hands looked, imagining what it would be like to touch them; to hold them.

Fuck. That was my next thought.

The possibility of being a faggot was terrible to me. And I say that because that is what I called myself. For most of my middle school years, despite being the good kid, I was also relentlessly made fun of by a handful of guys at school. Looking back on it, I've always been dripping in glitter. Even if I couldn't see it, other people could. My femme tendencies and a voice to match was an easy target for bullies and gossip queens. Couple that with my grossly inadequate sex education, I had to look up half of the stuff they said to me to figure out exactly how they were insulting me. Now, here I was in high school, and I was everything they said I was.

I can't be gay. I'm a Christian.

That was the line immediately running in my head, terror filling me wholly and instantly.

I was scared of everything I heard about gay folks. It was all sexual deviancy and ending up with AIDS and dying alone. It was living far from God. It was a sin that was a threat to the family. It was being in open rebellion against the King of Kings, and at the end of time, when judgment day arrived, I would wonder where I'd end up.

I loved Jesus and, apparently, I also had this thing, this attraction to boys, that I definitely did not choose but had no idea what to do with.

The bell rings. I snap back into the present and realize that I've been staring into space in his direction for a while, and he noticed. I took a sharp inhale, the kind where the breath rushes into your lungs because you've forgotten to breathe due to shock. But I wasn't looking at him. I was looking into what I perceived to be a dark and damned future.

I felt disgusting. I felt sad. I felt like I couldn't tell anyone.

But like any good Christian, I prayed about it. Because that's what I was taught to do when I was fearful.

What was interesting is as I took this to God in prayer, I reasoned with myself and the Spirit, and realized something true: I didn't choose to be attracted to boys. I know I didn't choose this. And if I didn't choose it, the only other logical option, to me, was that God designed me this way. When I asked the Holy Spirit to confirm it through feelings of peace, and if it wasn't right to give me discomfort (I know. It's super old school to ask for signs. I was a very pious kid.), what I felt was peace.

10

Peace that God loved me for who I am.

Peace that God would never leave me.

Peace that maybe I would find love one day, and it would make these feelings of shame worth it.

I told one person, and then a few other friends at school, keeping it a secret from most everyone for about a year. One arbitrary afternoon, my father and I got into a fight about what I wanted to study in college. And by fight, I mean *he* yelled at *me*.

I just sat at the kitchen table, as he stood there and told me that studying theatre would get me nowhere. It didn't matter if it was my dream to teach theatre. He said that my happiness wasn't necessary, that being employable was. It became evident that what was important to me, what I held close to me, wasn't safe with him. I couldn't ever tell him. I went to my room and cried for everything I was feeling. Being misunderstood and feeling alone because I know that I could never tell him I was gay. There was no way he could handle that if he couldn't handle me wanting to study the arts.

He later came upstairs and gave me the only apology he would ever give me the course of his fifty-eight-year life. Then began a line of questioning about why I was so upset about our conversation. I think he knew he struck some kind of deeper nerve with me.

"Are you having problems at school?" *No. I'm a good student, and you know that.*

"Is there someone giving you a hard time?" *I'm not about to tell you that.*

"Is it a problem with drugs?" *Wow.*

"Is it a problem with girls?" *Obviously not.*

"Is it a problem with sex?" I didn't say anything, and I'm relatively sure I stopped breathing again. That's been my physical response to stress since I was young.

"Kevin, are you gay?"

I was fighting back the tears and stifling the sobs that were begging to be let out. And, with a very stern and controlled voice, I said, "Kinda."

I was kinda gay. I didn't even identify that way at the time, but I didn't know what was going to happen next if I said I was, and I was scared. Would he beat me? Would he throw me out? The silence between us was pregnant, and at any moment, the water was going to break. Whatever this new thing was, we'd have to deal with it.

"I love you, and nothing is going to change that." I cried silently, but still, I couldn't look at him. I didn't believe him. "I think we should tell your mother."

Bad idea. The worst fucking idea, in fact. My mother was a very involved church member, she was a respected woman, I knew where she stood with this, and I knew her reaction wasn't going to be pretty. But he told her anyways. After she ran to the nearest Lifeway and picked up the first book she could find on homosexuality and the Bible, she informed me that we were going to beat this, as if it were cancer to cut out. And she said something that frightened me.

"Don't make you make me choose between you and God. You know who I am going to pick."

I knew that it wasn't me. Now the choice was myself or my family, my sin or my family. I was fourteen in a white-passing military family. Loyalty was bred into me and I would do anything, fighting enemies both foreign and domestic, to protect what was mine.

Mere days later, we were sitting in a biblical counsellor's office. Not a therapist, mind you, but someone with whom we had to sign a release form that we acknowledged that they weren't a trained therapist. As I sat across from this woman with a mom haircut, next to the dusty artificial plants, I cried and told this woman that I didn't want these feelings anymore. I didn't wanna lose my family, and I didn't wanna lose God, but I didn't know what to do.

She told me that I was right: I didn't choose this. However, I could decide how to respond to those feelings and desires. Being attracted wasn't the sin. Acting on them was. This was revolutionary for me. Who I was, at my core, was good. It was just my sin nature that is causing me to feel these things. It was the sins versus me. It was my father's fault for not affirming me at critical moments in my childhood. Apparently, that may have caused a perceived lack of masculinity, thereby manifesting unhealthy attractions towards people who possessed the masculinity I desired for myself (i.e. men). It was the sins of my mother, who was must've been too overbearing and let me become a soft mama's boy. I wasn't to blame.

They taught me it was my parents' fault. The thing is, despite my father's severity as a person, overall, he was incredibly loving throughout my childhood. My mother wasn't overbearing. In fact, she supported my love of theatre and music so much, never missing a show and always encouraging my artistic side. Justin Lee, the author of *Torn*, said it best in a talk he gave one time: "I couldn't find any problems until I went looking for them." And what we seek, we tend to find, do we not?

I bought into this bad theology because what was promised to me was the path to life. I bought it because it offered a specific issue, a clear cause, and a clear solution. I could become the man God intended me to be. This would fix the problem. Eventually, maybe, if I were faithful, God would change me; that I could rid myself of my sin nature. I was going to be a good Christian. Even if it killed me.

...

My first time sitting in a Living Waters meeting, which was an offshoot of Exodus International, I remember the pastor saying, "It is worth everything to commune with God." I've never forgotten it because it proved to be more accurate than I could ever imagine. In his mind, the pastor was saying it's worth the suffering. It's worth the pain of loneliness. It's worth foregoing all good pleasure and the things you think you need to be fully alive to be with God. After this brilliant and beautiful poetry, he began to point out how our deviant sexuality was a product of the fallen state of man, and a bunch of other shit that I have since unlearned and put out of my mind.

Twelve years of men's groups and ex-gay men's meetings and ex-gay conferences birthed in me a zeal to be a man after God's own heart. I was committed to this, and I was persuaded this was the best thing for me: this was the way I could honor God with my life. If I did the right thing, it should produce the correct result, right? However, my attraction towards men didn't go away. My sexuality never changed. How I approached building those relationships did.

I had plenty of good guy friends, all of whom were straight because God forbid I fall in love with them, and we fall into sin. But that provision in my own management of my sin didn't account for the fact that desire cares little about what you want to be true. Desire only *speaks* what is true.

I desired to be seen and known. I wanted to have someone affirm the goodness in me. I desired sex (obviously in the context of marriage because I was so holy). Though I desperately wanted these things to be with a woman, I never felt that compulsion. I wanted to. I sometimes could will it into existence. I had a few girlfriends, but it was always pretty shallow and pretty dull on my end. I mean, how many coffee dates where you hold hands and talk about your feelings can you get before someone gets bored? (Answer: at least six-months worth).

When I couldn't get my legitimate needs met, I tried to get my needs met in illegitimate ways. My desire for intimacy and companionship manifested self in a string of male best friends with whom I became obsessed. We were best friends, together all the time, doing life together. We would be the true definition of Christian Brotherhood. As soon as they found a girlfriend, I would withdraw, accusing them of changing or putting a woman before his friends (shout out to the patriarchy for that one). Granted, their patterns of behavior did change because the newness of relationships can be a vortex for two new lovers. But my reaction to them wasn't out of concern that they would become enmeshed and codependent. I was jealous.

Their attention was no longer on me, and I wasn't their emotional rock anymore. I had these expectations of my best friends that I never communicated because my view of myself was so unhealthy. It never occurred to me that the way I attached to people was directly linked to my trauma.

After my first semester of college, my father decided to divorce my mother. I went bananas a bit in the aftermath of that social explosion. I told God to fuck off and settled for a while to do whatever I wanted. Obviously, what I was doing wasn't working. I had done everything correctly. I prayed, fasted, dated women, and didn't kiss no guys, and I still wasn't less gay at all. I felt like I wanted a break from myself, or at least the self I had been trying so hard to be. I needed to not care. In fact, I couldn't care. There were zero fucks left to give. It wasn't that I was mad at God. I just became indifferent.

I dated precisely one guy in college and kissed many others. Honestly, I spent most of my time in college oscillating between being incredibly repentant for my homosexual desires and giving myself to them completely. I partied and fooled around with anyone I felt like and then had this dubious feeling of "I know that I should feel bad about this, but I don't. Why don't I feel bad about my sin?" That felt even worse than actually doing the deed itself. Was I so far gone in my sin that I couldn't even recognize what was holy anymore? I mean, I didn't think so, but isn't that what the sinful heart would say?

You see how that circular logic of shame works? It keeps us circling the question rather than taking action to figure out what the answer to the problem is. And the question is, "Is this true?"

Chapter 1

Shame within our faith operated as guardrails for us for so long. Derived from a belief in the separation between God and humanity, our parents and foreparents merely recreated the law, not believing the gospel of Christ, that in Jesus, the law was fulfilled. It is from a sincere desire to please God that we splinter ourselves, seeing only suffering as the means by which grace can be received. But this is an illusion. It isn't true.

So, I doubled down on my own fundamentalism. I joined a Pentecostal congregation that had tongues and expressive worship and phenomenal opportunities for community (if you could drink the Kool-Aid). I hopped on the worship team, and I became a bit of a zealot (again). For three years, I invested in a community that loved me and held space for me to overcome my struggles with homosexuality. They could speak my true nature into me because they just knew God. I trusted them. With their support, I was sure that this time, with the power of the Holy Spirit alive in me, I could kill this part of me. However, in the quiet of my mind, when I could stop and be honest, I didn't want this.

I didn't want to be straight. I had spent a few years kissing boys and I still remember what that felt like. It was a moment when my whole body lit up with electricity and passion and a surge of want. It felt like fireworks. It felt like a rush, and it felt like pleasure, and it felt like "Yes, this is it. This is what I've been missing." It was like a puzzle piece fell into place. I could finally see the whole picture. Yet my faith and my faith family was telling me that these pieces that fit perfectly into my frame were not right. By extension, they said *I* was not right.

One night at a men's group, I lamented that I didn't want healing bad enough. I didn't want to be straight and I no longer felt bad about it. And I felt bad about not feeling bad. So, what did that mean? Where did I stand in God's eyes? Was my rebellious heart going to land me in hell? Also, what good was heaven later if I was living in hell now? How could a promise of something better later heal me in the present? The struggle every day to not "give into my flesh" left me so tired and so angry all the time. I shared this with them, and my straight group leader said, "I get it. I understand."

"No, you fucking don't," I said without missing a beat. "Unless you wake up every day and you want to have sex with men, you don't know what it's like. Unless you have woken up every day of your life, hoping that something might strike you dead so you can be free of this feeling, you don't understand what I've been through."

I wish I could have held onto that fire because I was onto something. My experience told me something different than what the church was telling me. My experience told me that my connecting romantically with genders like my own was a good thing, that it was natural, innate. My church said that my feelings were incompatible with God's plan for men, women, and marriage. My question should have been, "Well, who decided what God's plan is?"

But in my desperation, I simply asked, "So what should I do?" I was told to hold on. Eventually, God would give me a miracle. My group leader prayed for me and prophesied over me. (If you're unfamiliar with this practice, it's basically a charismatic practice of speaking things into existence by naming the future you wish to see or the future you believe God is giving you a vision for. It's as wild as you think it is.) He told me that I was going to get married to a woman. He saw it. She was beautiful. Later in the vision, he saw me holding my son in the delivery room. Then he saw my son getting married. "He never had to deal with your struggle because you did your job as a father."

I sincerely wish I was kidding about this, but this was the moment I clung to like it was Jesus speaking directly to me. I didn't need to understand how. I need only believe. I didn't need to know why. I didn't need to understand the reason I was going through this or the reason I had to suffer for the kingdom this way, but it would all be worth it for the glory of God. (Also, what the fuck does that even mean?)

I trusted this man. Why wouldn't I? He loved me. He provided me with spiritual direction. He gave me a place to belong. So, I took him at his word, and held on tight. I once again kept myself from forming any relationships with other queer people. I pursued any opportunity to serve the church. Because if I was faithful and filled myself up with the Holy, the unholy couldn't be present. That's what I believed.

When the opportunity came up for me to go on this really long 11-month, 11-country mission trip, and you bet your self-righteous ass that I applied faster than anything else I've ever done. The program and organization boast the opportunity to experience discipleship through journey, giving you the tools to not just transform the world, but really transform yourself into the person God always meant for you to be. Their branding is impeccable, and when I applied and got accepted to the program, I didn't hesitate to drop all my other plans to make it happen.

Grad school applications were withdrawn. Auditions for Master of Music programs were canceled. I heard the call to saddle up my horses and go do this thingy for Jesus.

Chapter 1

The organization I went with leaned Pentecostal and Charismatic for sure, emphasizing gifts of the Holy Spirit. We were taught to expect miracles. Expect to have blind eyes opened. Expect healings to occur. Expect to encounter demons that you'll drive out. Expect (and this is my favorite) to find a spouse if you're faithful enough.

Though I wish I could confess total piety in my desire to serve God on the mission field, it would be dishonest of me not to share that the prospect of finding God's perfect match for me while serving the kingdom was incredibly appealing. I knew it would take a miracle. This was, in some ways, my last-ditch effort to fix myself.

My trainers told stories of folks who met at training camp, served together and fell madly in love. On top of that, we had people who stood up and told us how God delivered them from their homosexual desires into "full sonship." The passage one speaker shared was from the gospels. Jesus asks a man paralyzed from birth who is sitting by the healing pool, "Do you want to be well?" I cried the whole time he was talking because my soul was screaming, "Yes, Jesus. I want to be well. I want to be healed."

Can you imagine how I felt? Sitting there at a training camp in the backwoods of Georgia. Twelve years of struggle, plenty of years of faithful service, hungry for the things of God, and also really fucking lonely and desperate for God to do anything. If God could do those wild things, the blind eyes opening and demons being driven out, if God was still doing those miraculous wonders, there wasn't any reason why God couldn't finally fix me. After all this time, after doing the right thing, surely, I could meet someone on the mission field that would be the answer to my prayers.

Much to my chagrin, sleeping in the tent, eating off five dollars a day, and getting sick for the Lord didn't exactly produce the joy and holiness I was hoping for. It certainly didn't provide any heterosexual feelings whatsoever. In fact, I had made out with a guy I met in our travels. He was a Serbian college student, and we went walking by the river. He said, "I want to kiss you." I didn't stop him. It felt both thrilling and horrifyingly enjoyable to me.

Why didn't I feel bad about this? Again, I felt terrible about not feeling bad, not that I actually had committed my gay sin. I kept this secret from my team, of course, but the secret festered in my chest until it boiled up in the most inopportune moment.

2
WHO DO YOU SAY THAT I AM?

Four months into this eleven-month journey, our entire squad of fifty missionaries (using that term loosely) sat in this soccer complex somewhere in Kathmandu, Nepal. Our newly appointed squad leader, who was our age and was our peer just weeks before, got up and preached a beautiful sermon. He was well spoken; thoughtful. After the trip, he was Harvard bound. His sermon was very Presbyterian (which I didn't appreciate until later), and I couldn't even tell you what it was about. Still, I can remember what it triggered in me.

I felt this intense feeling of, "I don't fucking believe any of this. I can't keep lying about believing it either." I started crying, then sobbing, and then I tried to leave the room only to be met by a friend in the hall. I fell down flat on my face, my vision blacking out. I was conscious, but everything in my body was tension and chilling fear. My fingers contorted, my ears were ringing, my body was spasming, and I didn't know if I was on the ground for thirty seconds or thirty years. I couldn't move.

My friend got me off the ground and helped me walk down to the bus. I was panicked and still sobbing. I did the only thing I knew how to do. I asked God for help.

Our Father, who art in heaven,
Hallowed be thy name...

My breath slowed down on the ride back to our hostel. My friend got me something to eat and told me very plainly he believed that demons were attacking me. That assertion felt strange to say the least. I had similar things happen before in college, not to the same intensity. However, it felt familiar enough that I knew what I'd just experienced was probably an intense anxiety and panic attack. I think being on the mission field, trying to be good for God, and God still doing nothing free or heal me from my unwanted attractions, broke me. I was hurting so much, and I felt ashamed that I couldn't be stronger for God. I was a disappointment.

Despite the warning signs, despite my body telling me this was too much, despite my desire stating very clearly, "*I do not want to be here!*" I stayed. Because that was the "right" thing to do. If I wanted to be healed, if I wanted to be a good Christian, this is what it was going to take. Wasn't it worth everything to commune with God?

...

I stayed a lot longer on the mission field that I should have. After kissing one of the college boys I was supposed to be ministering to in Serbia, and then later dancing with boys on New Year's Eve, I began to think very clearly about killing myself. I kept reflecting on the final moments of Jesus, thinking of how he gave his body up so that others might live. "The Spirit is willing, but the flesh is weak." That's what he said to his disciples on the mount of olives the night he was betrayed. I felt that. I knew that I wanted to be healed. But also, my body wanted something else.

My flesh was the problem. Flesh itself was the problem. If I was going to sin and cause others to fall into sin, wouldn't it be better for me to stop myself before it happened? Would it be better for the world if I just wasn't here? There were so many moments where I could've just stepped in front of the buses in the busy streets. There were so many nights where I'd get drunk on cheap beer and stare off into the ocean like it was calling me.

I was in so much pain and, in my head, the only way to atone for my sexual sin was to stop the thing causing me to sin. I had to stop my body from sinning.

That's where my head was at. That was bad theology. And it dressed itself up in poetry and a promise that if I did something, if I did this one thing, God would finally not be mad at me.

When it got it got to be too much, I finally shared it with our squad

19

coaches, the two folks who were in charge of our spiritual formation in some ways. I told them how I was feeling; how I was struggling. They said to me that they believed that on the other side of this, God would bless me. They told me this is how the enemy works. Something in me, maybe it was my camp counselor training from back in the day, threw up a red flag.

When someone tells you that they've thought about how they might kill themself, you take immediate action to make sure they are safe. You don't qualify it or spiritualize it. You don't weigh them down with platitudes. You tell them you're here. You're listening. That you believe them and, more than anything, that you love them and will be with them.

I realized in an instant if I wanted to survive, I had to get the fuck out of there. I pulled out my credit card, bought a flight home, and informed my leaders I was leaving. I was done. This was not up for debate or negotiation.

My team understood, and two days later, on a Tuesday, they took me to the airport and hugged me good-bye.

And I left.

...

I felt a sense of relief, knowing that I was going to get help. And at the same time I had an equal and opposite feeling of dreadful guilt for leaving my squad. Guilty for failing my supporters who funded the trip. Guilty because I was failing my team. Guilty because I was coming home with my tail between my legs.

Guilty. Guilty. Guilty.

I failed.

Even though I was on the brink of suicide, even though I was doing what I needed to so that I could stay alive, it was *I* who felt the shame. My suffering was my fault. God was punishing me for my sins. This depression, this hoplessness, it was all because I wasn't trusting God enough, not loving God enough. That's what all the voices of my ex-gay therapists said, and their voices were cawing in my ear like in that creepy ass Hitchcock film, The Birds.

That feeling of failure compounded my feelings of shame around my sexuality. Within two months of being home, I attempted to kill myself.

Twice.

When I woke up the second time, realizing that I had once again failed at another thing, I did something I hadn't done before.

I wondered if I might be wrong. Because if I had survived this long, despite my best efforts, maybe there was a reason for that? Maybe God was keeping me alive for something? I didn't know. However, I was confident that I couldn't continue to live like this. I couldn't continue fighting a war inside. It consumed every most part of me. It created tension my body, disease my mind, and a longing for death in my spirit. Divorced from myself and my emotions, I lived only in extremes and bouts of trauma, and I was tired. I needed an answer.

Or instead, I needed better questions.

But where does one go to ask about impossible?

Well, any good millennial, I turned to the most excellent source of knowledge. Google.

Search terms: Can you be gay and Christian?

Immediately, I found a video where a skinny white boy laid out a very plainly how the Bible could be interpreted to include and affirm LGBTQ folks. I instantly thought he was preaching heresy and was almost offended that he could so flippantly use the Bible to fit the narrative he wanted. That is what my people, the leaders I respected, said about people like him.

At the same time, I wanted it so desperately to be true. I kept digging and found organizations, bloggers and just everyday folks on Twitter, living openly queer Christian lives. Some people lived in God-honoring marriages and, believe it or not, possessed love and joy *and* peace. They had abundant lives. At the same time, they made space for folks who disagreed: Other queer people who, like me, held to the standard of what we'd always known, that the Bible was clear about what marriage was and what it wasn't.

These questions began to ruminate in me.

What if I was wrong?
What if there were many ways to look at scripture?

I mean, we already did that in the Christian faith, and who's to say that these Queer folks couldn't also seek the Holy Spirit's guidance in this?

This was a tiny thread in the tapestry of my faith that I began to tug on. Could I be wrong? And God, how I wanted to be wrong. I didn't tug very hard, though. It took me two years before I really began to make a yank big enough to rip the seams of my life open.

Shortly after my second suicide attempt, and after discovering all these new queer and trans Christians on the Internet, I decided to *really* seek God's voice, just to make sure I gave it the old college try. Again.

I decided to intern at with the same organization that sent me as a missionary. You might be thinking, "Kevin, weren't they low key abusive to you?" Yes, they were. And I was trauma bonded to them. In my head, they still had the answers. My body yearned to be held in its questions. They were, in my heart, the only place who would understand me.

I joined their discipleship program, which was less of a discipleship program and more of a "you raise money to work for us, but you're never going to see that money" kind of internship. We had a lot of emotional worship sets, weekly charismatic speakers, training camps of more missionaries coming through before deployment, countless nights of inner healing, and we "did life together."

By "did life together," I mean, we would continuously blur the standard social lines between work life, personal life, social life, and spiritual life so severely that emotional and spiritual abuse happened widely and frequently. Most of the time, the ones on the receiving end of that abuse were made to believe that it was our fault. We weren't finding "Truth." And if we rocked the boat in one area, we rocked it in all areas. I remember having a conversation with someone questioning whether we interpreted scripture correctly. Within a day, I had texts and emails from my supervisor, my spiritual mentor, my house dad, and four other interns who wanted to get coffee with me to talk about how my walk was going.

At first, I was so bought in. I was here for the miracles (again). I just *knew* being in a place surrounded by God's people would be where I'd find healing. Surely this would be the place where maybe I'd find this woman who would be the proof of God's healing in my life. Ya know, when you look hard enough for something, sometimes you find it. Knock. Seek. Ask. That sorta shit.

Literally, the prettiest, most femme goddess of a woman flirted with me on my first day in my internship, and I flirted back. I won't lie, I'm a phenomenal flirt when I want to be. Within a few weeks, we were dating. Within a month, I was staying over at her place down in Atlanta. (And for the record, I stayed on an air mattress on the other side of her tasteful loft apartment because we were good Christians and sex is only good with Jesus if you make a bunch of promises that you'll undoubtedly break later and then maybe divorce. And heaven forbid you ever orgasm outside of trying to make a baby.)

Within five months, I was meeting her folks and looking at engagement rings because that, in my mind, was what Christian men did.

I really was drawn to her. She was artistic and generous and had excellent taste in so many things. I honestly loved being around her. We got along, and I'd say that she was, for a time, my best friend. That's what you look for, right? You look for that deep friendship because that's what matters in long-term relationships. Because after the sex is gone, you gotta still like each other! Honestly, I had no gauge for whether or not this what love for a woman felt and thought maybe this is how everyone feels. Just a strong affection for someone and respect. I just knew that it's what I was supposed to do. If I wanted to be a part of this community, then I should do what they do. This was the role I had to fill to belong, to be holy, for me to prove that I really was healed; that I really did love God.

On our drive up to meet her parents, it clicked with me that I loved her, but not in the way she deserved. I didn't want to marry her because I wanted to promise my eternal love for her. I wanted to marry her because I needed to be assured of God's infinite love for me. This was the pathway from my sin, and yet it required me to lie to someone I deeply loved and cared for. It was not honest.

I ended things shortly after we came back, but without telling her the whole truth. I felt her knowing I was gay would be embarrassing for her, mostly because I still wasn't okay with even saying I was gay out loud. I had to practice it. A week later, when I called her, it was only the third time I had said it with my actual lips. What I find mildly funny is that when I finally did tell her I was gay, and that's the reason we broke up, I recall her saying, "Oh, God... that makes so much sense."

We laughed, hung up the phone, and I started feeling a little better.

"I'm gay." I'd say it a dozen more times into the sticky Georgian air, waiting for a booming voice from above to shout me down, or the ground below my feet to open up and flames consume me. But neither happened. In fact, the only thing that opened up was my tear ducts. I wept, realizing for the first time that I had been right this whole time.

God really did love me. I couldn't do anything to change that.

...

It's been about four years since I came out, and I often joke with people that I feel like I've lived four lifetimes. So much has happened; jobs, lovers, faith evolutions and more profound questions. I've told my story on podcasts, through blogs, and in videos, and I can honestly say, there is no feeling more excellent than hearing my work has helped people stay alive. Because that's what I want. I want my people to stop killing themselves. I want violence against my people to end. Every bit of work I do, every breath in my being, is dedicated to seeing a world where queer folks are not afraid to be themselves, where Love is our law.

My work is centered around folks picking up the pieces of their faith that they still have left and make a pilgrimage across their River Jordan. To leave behind a broken faith system that never loved them, but only used them, leaving them hungry and thirsty. I have had countless moments in person, calls, emails, tweets, DM's from folks who have said that they are still alive because of a blog I wrote or a video I made.

I go to a local church and give my money when I can. I spend most of my time telling folks about how God loves them and wants them to live abundant lives. I work to train folks in community organizing to help empower them to be their own advocates. I coach people through their coming out process and through the reconstruction of their faith. I try to love people as much as possible. I own my mistakes. I apologize when I need to. I reconcile when I can. I really love Jesus.

I do not tell you these things to brag. I tell you these things because I want to ask you a question.

Who do you say that I am?

What does my life say about me?

What does my work and the results it yields say about me?

What do my practices say about me?

24

When you look at my story, how I have striven with God and with man, what does it say about me that I have fought to hold on to a faith tradition and stay in a church that wants, by and large, nothing to do with me. I believe it was Jesus who said that the greatest commandment was to love the Lord, your God, with all your heart, soul, mind, and strength, and the second is unto it: love your neighbor as yourself. So, who do you say that I am?

If you see the Christ and the teachings of Jesus... okay fine. I am "Christian."

If you see a human with kindness in his heart, then wonderful. I am a kind human.

If you see an unhinged person who is using liberal-minded theology that throws out the whole of scripture, two-thousand years of tradition, has the intention of ruining marriage, and practices a little casual magic... fantastic. I am an unhinged liberal-minded witch.

I really don't care what people call me anymore. I don't care if people identify me as a Christian. Frankly, it's not essential. Being validated in my faith journey one way or another does nothing to affirm or negate the truth of my experience of God. A person declaring whether I am in or out is invalid. For where is God's kin'dom if not the whole of the earth and the fullness thereof?

It doesn't fucking matter one bit what another human says about me, or whether they welcome me or not. I'll put myself on the outside because my people are out here. I don't give a fuck about being a part of the Church anymore. I give a fuck about following Jesus.

And he very might well be leading me out of what feels like a hellscape of a religious, social experiment gone terribly wrong.

...

Why am I telling you that story in particular? Why did I give you my big gay sob story at the front end of a book about bad theology?

I'm telling you my story because not everyone has survived to tell theirs.

I'm telling you my story so you can get just a glimpse of what I mean what I say when I say, "bad theology kills."

When I say, "bad theology kills," I mean, I attempted suicide twice. I mean, I spent most of my life hating myself and abusing my body with drugs and alcohol to numb the pain of my self-disgust. I mean that on the other side of therapy and two years of meds, I still have days I doubt I want to live.

When I say, "bad theology kills," I mean that every day somewhere, there's a queer kid who is getting picked on by someone else, and that queer kid is going to think about jumping from that bridge, pushing that knife just a little deeper than they did the last time, eating whatever pills from their cabinet they find and not waking up.

When I say, "bad theology kills," I mean that there are still countries in our world who outlaw queer relationships and expression and punish it with death. Many of these countries were influenced heavily by Christian money.

When I say, "bad theology kills," I mean that unarmed black people are getting shot by police and facing zero consequences.

When I say, "bad theology kills," I mean that trans women of color are being massacred and no one is talking about it.

When I say, "bad theology kills," I mean that babies are being ripped from their mothers' arms, humans trying to flee from terror are being put in cages at the border, and a president is allowing it to happen.

When I say, "bad theology kills," I mean that a white man walked into a black church in Charleston and killed nine black people with a gun, a teen walked into a high school in Florida and killed seventeen people with an assault rifle, a man walked into a gay club and killed forty-nine brown queer people with an assault rifle, a man walked into Sandyhook elementary and killed twenty babies and six adults with a gun.

When I say, "bad theology kills," I mean that the US government cares more about protecting a single cell in a human body than it does about the woman who was raped.

When I say, "bad theology kills," I mean that there is an alarming number of missing indigenous women, and no one can find them.

When I say, "bad theology kills," I mean that families are kicking kids out of their homes when they tell them about who they are.

When I say, "bad theology kills," I mean that Leah Alcorn stepped in front of a semi-truck on the highway because her family wouldn't call her by her name.

When I say, "bad theology kills," I mean that

bad theology is
killing
all
of
us.

And.

A better way is possible.

INTERLUDE I
A STATEMENT OF FAITH

I believe everything and I believe nothing. I believe that God is real, that God isn't real, that God is beyond real. Just as the Universe is boundless and ever-expanding, going on without end, there is God in the vast foreverness that is infinity. And we cannot understand. We can never grasp things without boundaries or without form or without rules. We can never understand what it is to be free and uninhibited. But I believe we can have a taste of that bliss, that joy, that pleasure.

I believe that it's likely that all this is probably some weird, magical, mystical, happy accident. The theory is that somewhere around 13.8 billion years ago, there was a mass of infinite density, weight, pressure, and contained within it was everything that would become anything. Within it was all manner of possibility, of magic, of questions, of creativity, of beauty, of life. And as that's the best working theory, I suppose I believe for now.

I'd imagine that mass of everything thought unto Themself, "I wonder what I am here for... let's find out." Perhaps they said, "I wonder what *We* are here for."

And so suddenly They decided to be everywhere, and everywhere which They were not, They then went and were.

Then like things started moving closer together, forming gases and rocks and weird space dust until explosions and fire and gravity began moving like particles closer and closer together. Fast forward. The conditions were right, and now here we are: expressions of whatever it was at the very beginning

28

who had a question about why it was here.

Humans.

Made with all the same stuff as supernovas and stars and planets and galaxies. As our minds began to evolve, from the moment we could notice ourselves thinking, we've wondered how we could even think in the first place. We've wondered how. We've wondered why. These are the greatest Mystery.

People gave the Mystery many names and worshiped Them as a plethora of deities. They developed ways of communing with the Mystery, with ritual and myth and ceremony. As the world shared with itself the different iterations of God, some began to realize that everyone was talking about the same thing, the same source, the same creative force, the same energy, the same beginning. We've been singing different melodies about the same subject.

The only differences are the rituals, the languages, the lore, the tools, and the practices. Still, it all points to the same truth:

Nothing real can be threatened.
Nothing unreal exists.
Herein lies the peace of God.[3]
And if you can see the reality of God in yourself, you will see it everywhere, in everything, through everything, with everything.

All of everything is an expression of God's curiosity to see what everything might become. The fact that anything is anywhere begs the question for me, "*How?* How is it all staying together?" Science tells us that it's atoms, reationships of energy on such a small scale that we are literally a universe of moving energy.

But what is it?

I think it's "God." That thing that's on the tip of my tongue that only poetry and music and feeling and sex and sorrow and awe and wonder can capture. "God" is the experience of it all. "God" is the one experiencing it all here now through Me.

It's the answer at the question of "How?" God. Love. The Universe. Me

---

[3] *A Course In Miracles*, Introduction

You. It's all the same. It's that thing that makes you cry when you hear music or your baby cry for the first time. It's the reason you see the sun set at Laguna Beach a thousand times and still there is something magical and majestic about it. There is a pulse rushing through everything, a deep sense of knowing beyond knowing, though the Universe is vast, ever-expanding and limitless, that we are connected to it all: to the source, the beginning, to what we would call God.

I believe we can only speak in God in metaphors. I believe that all religion, at its highest level, points us God in each other and calls us to love, honor, and respect that divinity present in all created things.

I believe Jesus was a man who was so connected to God, so attached to Love, one with divinity, but no more than you or I. His mind was completely healed by the Holy Spirit, knowing beyond mere belief that there was no separation. The only difference between Jesus and his followers, both initial and present-day, was/is an awareness of that unity. Jesus wanted everyone else to feel the same thing. Because Jesus has done it, giving us the example of right living with place and people, we see our potential in these incarnated bodies is nothing less than transcendent bliss in divine union with All.

Because we have equal access to Love, we see in Christ our own potential for a full life.

I believe Jesus wanted to start a movement, to show people that there was a better way of being human and that it is our inherent divinity which leads us toward our best self, toward life abundant. I think Jesus probably would have balked at the idea of starting a religion in his name. I believe Jesus was real, and because I remember him in the Bread and the Cup, Jesus is alive.

I believe the Holy Spirit is just another name of the pulse that runs through everything and holds it all together.

I believe that Love is real, that my body is divine, and that nature reveals more of God than our conscious minds can perceive. I believe in my choices affecting my life as much as I believe the Universe is conspiring on my behalf. I believe the question of why we are here and why we exist to be irrelevant in light of the question of what we will do with the time we are given to us.

I believe that beauty is Love made manifest.

I believe that our intention creates magic, that the Divine speaks in our bodies, in whispers, impressions, in stars and signs, through crystals and passing thoughts and tarot cards and music and our friends.

I believe God is queer.

I believe I could be wrong about all of this.

An Explanation

I don't know how to talk about God. Which is weird, isn't it? Here I am, writing a whole book on how to think about God, or at least Christian faith, and I honestly couldn't tell you the first thing about God. Weird, right? That statement probably all sounded like a bunch of hippy-dippy, mystic mumbo jumbo, a load of new-age tainted, anti-theodicy, heretical, witchy non-sense. That's because it is hard to write about believing in something and not be sure about what you believe. It's where I am at right now: unmoored, floating under a full moon on an ocean of my own questions. No wind or movement. Just choppy waves and the question of how long I can stay out there before I'll die from dehydration, how long can I live without what I once considered the Water of Life.

Ironically, I do not feel far from God. In fact, I feel closer to God than I ever have in my life because I'm convinced that there is not a moment in existence when I am outside of God's presence because God's presence is as vast as the space between stars and as close as the atoms that make up my body.

So, while I feel so close to God, assured in God's love for me, the thing I feel unmoored from is actually the Church in nearly every single expression. I wonder if this experiment that was (supposedly) started by the disciples of Jesus has run its course, the results of this experiment, unfortunately, pointing to more damage in our world than any actual good. I wonder if it's relevant.

If it is to remain in this world, the Church must evolve into something better. It must become the organized religion that organizes around the *right* things, as Brian McLaren shared in his book, *The Great Spiritual Migration*. Organized religion is not the problem. It is when we organize around things that are valueless that we forget our prophetic voice. I believe it is possible for the Church to change because "change is the law of God's mind and resistance to it is the source of all pain."[4] It all depends on whether the Church is ready to renounce white supremacy, patriarchy, and power. Being

---

[4] Craig Ferguson, *The Late Late Show*

that the Church is made of people, and our species has evolved to love power and prize it about everything, even human life, I profess to have no hope to see a significant change in my lifetime. "Power concedes nothing without a demand."[5]

We've only begun demanding to be seen in our full humanity.

Community, Confession, and Communion

I wonder if I am still a Christian, mainly based on everything written above. I assume many would consider my practices anywhere from unholy to wild and blatant heresy. Most of the time, I want to give up the label of Christian. I want to walk away from the Church. But the reality is that even if I didn't have the Church, it's likely I'd still talk about God through the lens of Jesus. It's the tradition I've spent my whole life in, the one that I connect most with, the one that makes sense given my experience, and the one that introduced me to God. That gratitude keeps me here, for the moment at least.

I personally need the community that the Church provides for me. On my own, I'm rather terrible. I have impulse control, but I also have an insatiable lust for intensity. The Church holds me accountable to my best self and to the things I profess to believe in (which isn't much, but still). The Church reminds me that I am forgiven, that I don't need to be perfect, I just need to give a damn about people. The Church tells me that I am imperfect, and that I require people, that I need God, love, and forgiveness.

This confession that I am imperfect, that I have committed sins against God by sinning against others in word and deed, in words said and unsaid, in action and in inaction, allows me to be in community with others who recognize the same need for grace in themselves. The Church, at its best, is a community that is ready to admit its own sin and work to mitigate the suffering of others.

As we confess, we remember that on the night Jesus was betrayed, he told his best friends that God was for them and that there was going to be no separation anymore. He gave them bread and wine, saying it was his body and blood, saying that God was not so mysterious that God couldn't be found in our own bodies, saying that "God was not so grand as to not be present as something as simple as bread and wine" (-Rev. Emmy Kegler). Jesus was saying God is here, and there, and everywhere if we would just open our

---

[5] Frederick Douglas, 1857

eyes to see it.

Look at the birds! Look at the flowers! Look at them being birds and flowers. Look at them in their holy instant, as they are now. Just being here, being what and who they were created to be. Can you be like that? Can you see it?

The Bread and the Cup remind me that God is for me and always has been. The Eucharist tells me that grace is given, never taken. Communion tells me that there is a great cloud of witnesses proclaiming that they stand with me on my journey towards God. The Lord's Prayer reminds me that I am part of a tradition that dates back thousands of years and that people are still asking for the same things:

To feel connected to a benevolent Universe.
Enough for today.
A connection to the Eternal.
Earth as it is in Heaven.

3
DOING THEOLOGY BETTER

My first day in seminary, my Old Testament professor asked the class, "What is the Bible?" Being the progressive smart ass that I am, I raised my hand.

"It's a collection of sixty-six books," I began in a monotone, "Written over the course of thousands of years by multiple people in multiple scenarios and cultures, giving their account of their experiences with God." Pretty solid answer if you ask me. The next response from another student made my jaw drop.

"It's the living word of God."

Oh, honey, no, I winced. That's an answer I'd have given you five years ago, full of platitudes and loaded terms that carry a significant amount of baggage. Sure, maybe in a poetic sense, it's the Living Word of God™, but make no mistake; the Bible was written, compiled, and edited by humans.

Do you know where we even get the phrase "word of God?" It's what agents of Caesar would deliver to the conquered peoples. They brought the gospel, the good news of the empire, from Caesar, called the Son of God, to the people living under their rule. They declared, "Caesar is Lord." It was often said that these agents, in the Greek called *evangeleon,* carried the "word of God" in their proclamations.

Word of God. Gospel. Evangelism. Jesus is Lord. All things the early church used as a way to subvert the rule of those in power in very clever and bold ways that you miss if you take it at face value with no context.

The Bible isn't a guide to life, nor does it give us basic instructions before leaving Earth as your pastor would like you to believe. The Bible isn't basic, and it isn't all that clear on many things people claim it's decisive on. On top of that, and I'd argue most importantly, the Bible isn't "perfect." It's not the unchanging "word of God" in the way we'd like to think of it. (And, just for the record, the Bible wasn't written in English, so like... if that's a thing for you, just let that go.)

That's the thing so many people want square in their minds: Does being affirming of LGBTQ people mean that the Bible is wrong? And if the Bible is "wrong" then what role does my faith even play in my life? Great question, too. Because the Bible contradicts itself in so many places. If you were looking to this book to be a reliable and cohesive guide to life, you might be looking in the wrong place. Or perhaps you have just been cherry picking what verses you liked wanted to read.

Funny how humans do that, huh?

Here's the thing: you can love the Bible, and your queer friends. You can love the Bible and also take issue with it. And *if* you love the Bible, then you should question it. You should go deeper. You should be wrestling. You can love the Bible and also think that women should be equal in the Church, that guns should be harder to attain, that healthcare should be universal. It is possible, and there are hermeneutical devices that can guide you and help you back-up your position. But your hermeneutics aren't the problem. Instead, your approach to the Bible might be.

A lot of Evangelicals tout having a "Biblical worldview" and usually hold that as the golden standard of what it means to be a Christian. The issue comes when trying to have any sort of meaningful dialogue with someone who cannot see the Bible for what it actually is. Furthermore, because their view of what the Bible is, any conversation surrounding morality becomes tenuous and tends to breakdown rather quickly.

When you begin to really press "Bible-believing" Evangelicals on where we get our morality from, they usually have a few answers.

One of them may be that we derive our morality from God, or at least the God we see in the Bible. Which, if you've read the Bible at all, feels a little confused. On the one hand, we have all these depictions of God through the prophets as a loving father and husband, and we hear in the New Testament

35

that God is love itself. But at the same time, there exist these horrific accounts where God orders the genocide of the Canaanite people. Literally. God ordered the murder of all the men, women, and children.

There's one fun story in the Bible from 2 Samuel where God incites David to take a census. What's odd though is that taking a census was against God's command to *not* take a census, because a census was always associated with how many able-bodied men David could call up into an army. It was about measuring your military strength and assessing whether you could flex it. God warned the nation of Israel not to become war profiteers like other nations, and this may have been the first inkling of a move toward Israel's empending empire building.

And what was God's response to David taking a census after God incited him to take said Census? Being a gracious God, David is given a choice between three years of famine in the land, three months of being on the run from his enemies, or three days of plague. David can't stand to make that choice, so God decides for him and sends *a plague*, killing seventy-thousand people.

God punishes David for being obedient. You don't even need a very close reading of the text to pick that up. Isn't that wild? How come nobody taught us this in high school bible study? But wait! We haven't even gotten to the best part.

What kind of asshole dad tells his child to do something and then punishes them for doing that thing? (Answer: an abusive one.)

This story is later retold in 1 Chronicles 24, and this same story says that Satan incited David to take the census. For those of y'all keeping score at home, that's a glaring contradiction of God's character within the Bible itself followed up by another account which blames Satan and not God, clearing God of all wrong doing and meriting the punishment of killing seventy-thousand people for David's sin.

So which one is true? The first or the second one? Both of them? Because I was told the Bible is clear my whole life and this seems like a pretty obvious contradiction, wouldn't you say? I could go on and read the entirety of the Bible for filth if I wanted, but that's not my point. My point is that we should be asking how the hell do we derive any morality or moral authority from a book that clearly has so many moral issues with the main characters and the contradictions it has in the text itself?

If we can't derive our morality from the picture of God we find in the Bible, and we also can't use the Bible in and of itself as a source of morality with it obvious moral failings when held against modern sensibilities and, ya know, human rights, then what? Where does one find out what is most moral or actually True with a capital T?

When we are using our critical minds, we can see that the Bible is anything but basic instructions. The Bible is a collection of stories across the centuries of different peoples and persons trying to describe their experience of God.

I think we have to see our own experiences of God the same way. Why should we. think that our stories and experiences of God are any less valid than the ones we read in the Bible? What disqualifies us from making claims about the nature of God and reality and Love? In fact, I'd say we are more qualified to make those calls than the writers of the Bible because, to be frank, they are not here. We are. We have to live with the reality of our own beliefs and theologies, not Paul or Martin Luther or Augustine or any voice from the grave. Us. We are the ones who are eating the fruit of a 2000 year old tree, and it's largely poison.

There is no way that the writers could have predicted the sheer number of technological, social, and scientific advancements that got us to the present dumpster fire of a world.

I don't think the Bible is perfect. But I don't need it to be. I need it to be a source of wisdom. I need it to be a song of peoples who came before me, who were asking the same deep existential questions as you and I.

Who am I?
What am I doing here?
Who is God?
What is God?
Where is God?

When I can suspend my need for it to be anything other than what it is, I am much more equipped to navigate my faith with resilience God's ever-changing world.

...

Rev. Broderick Greer, a Black, queer episcopal priest said, in one of the best keynotes I've ever heard, "While some do theology from the perches of power, some of us to theology as a form of survival." That's what it has been to me for so long. I had to learn to read myself into Biblical texts, to see myself in the story of Jesus if I had any hope of remaining a Christian, let alone remaining a part of the Church. In my experience, it is in doing theology that will move us from merely surviving to actual abundant life.

As I said, I'm not proof-texting the six clobber passages for you. You can google that. What I want to do is provide a framework for you to begin to ask better questions. If you're a theology nerd, you've probably already heard of this lovely little theological device that John Wesley, the founder of Methodism, gifted us when he was doing his thing.

It's called the *Wesleyan Quadrilateral,* and it's made up of four main sections: Tradition, Scripture, Reason, and Experience. It is a circle that feeds back in on itself, and all four are needed to make a really healthy, well-rounded, and well-informed spirituality.

Let's look at the traditional view of sex and marriage through the lens of the Wesleyan Quadrilateral. We'll take a look at how we use it to deconstruct this harmful theological view and begin to build a better theology in its place.

The traditional view of sex in marriage is that sex acts are reserved for one man and one woman in the confines of a marriage. Pretty standard, right? How many of us have attempted to hold up that standard and failed? 97% of us. 97% of people have sex before marriage.

How many of us did hold up that standard and were deeply wounded by the purity culture attached to it? How many of us held up that standard, got married and it was perfect until it wasn't? How many of our friends got married knowing fully well their partner was gay?

This teaching has hurt all of us, not just queer people and women. Though women and queer folk, I believe, have been more negatively impacted by these teachings. However, we all are affected by the separation it created between our minds and bodies. This separation extends in all directions, keeping us separated in a constant set of seen and unseen hierarchies, meaning someone is always on top and someone is always on the bottom.

The way faith understanding worked growing up, and I think still works in fundamentalist spaces, is in that order given above in the Wesleyan Quadrilateral. It has to begin in tradition, informing how we read and interpret scripture. How we read scripture then informs our reason and the framework through which we interpret our experiences. This is all well and good until our lived experience doesn't fit into the framework that has been constructed for us.

For me, realizing that I was queer was the experience that broke my framework. I was told my entire life that God loved me and hated sin, and that being a gay was very, very sinful. I was also told that sin is actions or inactions that hurt other people (which, if I am being honest, is a pretty good definition of sin, but we'll get to that later).

That's where I got hung up.

I was under the assumption that one willingly chose to sin. It was something did or left undone consciously. When I realized I was attracted to other boys, I hadn't "done anything" with a guy. The feelings came out of no where. Or rather, they came from somewhere deep inside me, like they had always been there.

But being gay is a sin, I'm told. But I didn't choose that. I for damn sure I didn't choose to be a gender transgressing homosexual in the American South in an Evangelical home. Who in their right mind would would choose that? Plus, I've never heard of a straight person choosing to be gay? Willingly changing their sexuality on a whim? By the logic of "sin is a choice and homosexuality is a sin therefore homosexuality is a choice," one should theoretically be able to just flip a switch and choose want something else.

But that's a farce of an idea, obviously. And that's where this conversation doesn't usually go in these so-called "loving-but-not-affirming" spaces.

Is sin about doing or being? Is sexuality an act or an identity?

I knew that I could stop myself from doing just about anything. Plus I was too scared of Hell to question any of this, or even see this breakdown in logic. I needed and yearned for belonging, safety, home. We all do. And so while I knew I wasn't *doing* anything wrong, I also believed that anything I did in my head was a sin, because of that whole verse where Jesus talks about committing adultery in your heart being just as bad as doing it. That wasn't his point, and the bad theology that was taught to me was "you are your thoughts, and if you have bad thoughts it is because you are bad. And you are bad because we're all sinners. And homosexuals are just the worst of them all."

People always say "love the sin and hate the sinner." But sexuality is part of our created being. So while perhaps well meaning and aimed at creating tolerance, what this does is create an internal shame narrative in Queer folks.

It's very clear logic.

Who I am is sinful.
God hates sin.
So, God hates me.
Because I am an abomination.

Can you imagine what it is like to hear your entire life that God hates you? Maybe not in so many words, and perhaps that's not exactly what they said, but that is what we heard. "God loves the sinner but hates the sin." This is where many conservatives get lost. This is where bad theology becomes deadly.

Sexuality isn't about who you want to stimulate your genitals on any given day. (I mean it is but also that's not the whole thing.) Sexuality is the desire to connect deeply, to know as you are fully known. It is how we perceive beauty in the world. It is how we form relationships and bonds, sexual, romantic, platonic or otherwise. It is how we create community and family. Ultimately, our sexuality is an expression of divine creativity and a desire to make Love manifest on the Earth.

When you hear your whole life that your sexuality is displeasing to the God of the Universe, to your Heavenly Father (whom you already see as pretty punitive because you grew up in a very narrow religious space), and being that your sexuality is deeply interwoven with your body, your spirit, and your essence, you can imagine how easy it is to fall into the belief that you, at your core, are bad.

We can go our whole lives, suffering under the same abuse and never realize that something better might be possible. We think suffering is our birthright and our glory. But it is not.

Wonder is.

. . .

As I said earlier, the experience that broke my religious box was my queerness. But initially, I took the theological route I always took because it's the one I knew.

My tradition says that "being a homosexual is bad, and here's why in the Bible." Because the Bible is a source of wisdom and authority according to my tradition, I must use it as *the* tool through which I interpret my experiences. I must use the Bible when I decide what is moral. This allows one to invalidate almost an innumerable amount of lived experiences with the phrase, "The Bible is clear about this."

Or so we're told.

For a time, I fit myself into the robust mental framework handed to me. And it worked. As long as my behavior didn't change, I was good. What this framework didn't account for, however, was desire. It did not consider that some people did could not fulfill this mandate to save sex for heterosexual marriage because we did not fall in love with a particular type of person. It did not account for any difference at all.

This version of marriage only serves what Black civil rights activist, essayist, and dope ass living prophetess, Audre Lorde, would call "the mythical norm".

The mythical norm is the set of identity markers of what we've been conditioned to see as "normal," which can be traced back to white colonialism. White colonialism, when it began to take over the world, tried to shape the world its image, making its rule and reign and power exertion over others normal. It is power that says something is normal. For too long, power has said that normal looks like a white, able-bodied, straight, heterosexual, cisgender, affluent male. It is why you see so many gay men shame one another for being femme. Even in our more liberated communities, we wear the shackles of a king that will never welcome us to his table. We have finally walked away from the table, but we crave the crumbs.

I wasn't normal. I was sitting at this table of heteronormativity but not getting fed. What I wanted, what my body craved, how my spirit longed to connect and be seen did not go away. I still was attracted to men. I needed to let love flow from me in a particular way, the way I was designed. My attraction to men caused me such mental distress and cognitive dissonance. A feeling of constantly policing my mind and presentation and the way I talked so that I didn't sound or look queer. My charge was to ride my body of sin, and that included my thoughts.

Hide. Suppress. Resist the thing that felt as natural as waking up. I was utterly erasing who I was, leaving nothing but a scared soul, clinging to a body like a one might cling to a life-raft in a hurricane.

...

Love only flows in two directions: in and out of a person. If you stop the flow of Love in any direction, you stop the flow in all directions. Stifling my sexuality was stifling my ability to give or receive love. Thus, I was stifling God's work in my life and any hope I had for a future.

So, in bringing back around to our good ole pal, the Wesleyan Quadrilateral, what is our experience of the teachings of our time?

Pain.

Pain was my experience of this teaching. My sound mind, my reason that God gave me, tells me that pain is bad. My body is telling me that this hurts and I should stop doing it. Wisdom traditions teach us that some suffering is inevitable, but undue suffering at our own hands? There is no wisdom in that.

And on top of that, I *want* to agree with what my body knows intuitively to be true. "But the Bible says..."

But what is the Bible? This is another one of those areas where I begin to lose conservatives because the Bible, to them, is the infallible word of God. To them, it is plain English, and if you can't handle what the Bible says, then you're just as a sinner and refuse to believe God's Truth with a capital T.

What I find amazing about this sentiment that Evangelicals have fostered over the past few decades is the belief that their interpretation is the *only* interpretation of scripture. Evangelicalism, the Southern Baptist Convention, and modern American non-denominationalism have only been around for the past seventy-six years, and they largely ignore the tradition and the two-thousand years of our history and how we've primarily argued about the holy texts and what they mean. We've had thousands of church splits over this. The most notable being the Great Schism of the Catholic Church in the west and the Eastern Orthodox Church, then later the Protestant Reformation. Here we are, five-hundred years removed from Martin Luther nailing *'95 Things I Hate About You*[6] to the Church door, calling out his tradition for the harm they were causing. In this, he entered into the same space as Jesus.

---

[6] It was actually called **Ninety-five Theses**, propositions for debate concerned with the question of indulgences, written (in Latin) and possibly posted by Martin Luther on the door of the Schlosskirche (Castle Church), Wittenberg, on October 31, 1517. This event came to be considered the beginning of the Protestant Reformation.

He entered into the dance of theology that folks had been doing since we could even wonder about the universe.

He got in the ring and decided to wrestle with God.

He did theology better in real time.

Now, let's not forget, Martin Luther was hella antisemitic. Some of his later works included a lovely little number by the name of *Jews and Their Lies,* wherein he suggested that one should burn down their synagogues. Like Paul, he was ahead of his time in so many ways and so bound by his time. He wanted liberation for his people from the tyranny of an empire and yet didn't see someone else as worthy of the same freedom. To me this feels like an early example of why non-intersectional justice movements always fail. Because they do not understand that when one is not free, none of us are free.

The Evangelical idea of Biblical literalism is a toxic theology that has made an idol out of a book. To say that you have access to absolute Truth is to say that you know the mind of God absolutely. And how could anyone? God is endlessly knowable. Biblical literalism is also academically dishonest. It contributes to a culture of fear and control by demonizing knowledge itself and delaying the liberation of peoples.

So, if the Bible is now up for interpretation, that leaves just one thing: Tradition.

What has my tradition, my faith, my family, my culture, my church said about sex and marriage. They've said that sex is to be saved for marriage based on Biblical reasons that we do not agree with. The answer is not to simply stop arguing and just capitulate to what they tell us to.

Hell to the no. Instead, I think we should try to be like Jesus.

...

In Luke 13, there is this story where Jesus goes into the temple on the Sabbath. A woman was present who was bent over because of an evil spirit was present. Jesus heals this woman, and she's instantly standing up straight and praising God. The religious leaders got pissed at Jesus, telling him that there are six days for work, but that the Lord has commanded them to keep the Sabbath holy.

Jesus' healing was breaking the law.

He said to them, "You hypocrites! Would not one of you on the Sabbath untie your ox or your donkey from the manger and lead them to water? Why should this daughter of Abraham, who has been oppressed by Satan for eighteen years, not be set free on the Sabbath!" [7]

The text says that these religious leaders were put to shame.

Okay, what just happened?

Jesus knows the law. He's a rabbi, after all. He knows what tradition and scripture say about working on the Sabbath, and so does everyone else there. But what was his experience?

His experience was he saw a woman suffering, and it was within His power to help her, and He did. His experience of suffering led to his reason, asking, "Is this right?" He knew the scriptures and the tradition wouldn't agree with Him. He did it anyway. He healed someone on the Sabbath, flying in the face of a tradition that was harming people in real-time.

He essentially looked at the pastors of the church He was at and said, "What the fuck is wrong with you? Y'all care more about your animals than you do about people suffering." Jesus was continually reimagining theology in ways that liberated.

In this, Jesus was living into the words of the prophet Isaiah when he said, "If you remove the yoke from among you the pointing of the finger, the speaking of evil, if you offer your food to the hungry and satisfy the needs of the afflicted, then your light shall rise in the darkness and your gloom be like the noonday."[8]

Jesus was looking at the leaders of his time and saying, "This yoke is too heavy. You've made it so hard for people to follow God." Jesus was continually doing theology this way, letting his experience drive him back to the question of how things could be better. Even He was wrong about something one time.

There's a story in the book of Matthew where a Syrophoenician woman rolls up on Jesus and pleads for the life of her daughter. Jesus says that he came for the Children of Israel, and to give bread to the dogs would be wrong, effectively telling this woman, "Back off, bitch, I'm not here for your

---

[7] Luke 13:15-16. NRSV
[8] Isaiah 58: 9b-10

trash people." He insulted her.

Yet, she persists. "Even dogs eat the crumbs from the master's table."[9] And Jesus changes His mind.

"Woman," He says, "Your faith is great. It shall be done as you wish." The woman's daughter was healed instantly.

This woman stood up and bore witness to her suffering. Jesus experienced her suffering, reasooned that suffering and pain should be mitigated whenever possible, and even though tradition would say demand He stay "pure" by disassociating from an ethnic group different than His own, in that moment Jesus chose to do the right thing. He did theology in real time. He looked at how His tradition and interpretation of scriptures let pain continue, saw it was wrong, and did something about it.

...

Now, what does this have to do with the traditional teachings on sex and marriage?

What the Church has historically and traditionally taught about human sexuality, and our worth has caused suffering and devastation to a generation of people. It is in the face of our experience of suffering, reasoning that the call of Love is to alleviate suffering whenever possible, we name it for what it is: suffering. It is causing people to feel separate from God, from their bodies, and from one another. As such, this bad theology and the praxis derived thereof are sinful.

If Jesus is the standard for which we are going to argue morality, then we should actually use Jesus as the standard. Jesus was compassionate. Jesus was taking the yoke off his people. It is compassion which the Church at large lacks towards those under the yoke of bad theologies that work only for the few and the privileged. It is time to end that suffering. Not only is it our right to argue with our tradition and those in it, but it is also our calling.

Our survival depends on it.

---

[9] Matthew 15:27

4
WHAT THE ACTUAL HELL?

It is so easy to forget what fear feels like; tastes like. It is either because I have not eaten of it in so long that I've forgotten the taste, or it is that I eat it so often that my tongue has lost its sensitivity to its electric sour smack. Something I was asked one time was how I was "so courageous." They were asking how they might also overcome their fear.

I'm not sure we ever get over fear. I think we learn to work with it, and in some ways perhaps ultimately become indifferent to it because its fearful dreams are merely a product of our own mind.

Meaning, if we recognize we are believing something is untrue, we do not have to believe it any longer unless we choose to. Our fear and anxiety about nearly everything can be undone in but a moment, for it is merely a changing of the mind, according reality its due while gently releasing our misperceptions.

After becoming cool with the whole God's cool with the gays thing, the next theology to crumble was all of it. It was truly a house of cards, and I pulled on the one labled "hell."

Hell wasn't making sense to me any longer, at least not as a place we could go when we died. I changed my mind and began to believe that God was infinitely pleased with me and that nothing could separate me from Love. It is in the presence of Perfect Love that fear is driven away, and I think that's how I know that I'm on the right track.

When I started getting into public work, though, I had to relearn what it was to feel fear at the beginning stages, before it's your dance partner and way before it ever becomes your friend. I had forgotten what it was to be afraid of being wrong. That's the secret question so many of us are carrying around in us.

What if we're wrong?

What if everything our shitty churches said is actually the truth, and we are really heathens? What if we are really going to Hell for rebelling against God's commandment for boys to not suck dick and girls not to grab boobies? What if there really is going to be a slide show of all my sins before God right before I'm sentenced to firey damnation but right before Krunk pulls the lever, I shit myself in front of God's holy court because I decided my last meal would be chimichangas?

I get it. Eternal conscious torment is a pretty shitty alternative to living in eternal life with God in Heaven. So, when someone tells you to pray a specific prayer, to accept Jesus into your heart so that you can avoid your soul literally burning up forever (for eh ver), what are you gonna do? Likely, if you're young and impressionable, and if this is the only narrative you were told, of course, you're gonna say the damn prayer. Of course, you're going to get in line. Of course, you are going to capitulate to whatever the people in charge are saying because they know better, right? They've been around longer, have the best in mind for you, and love you. They don't want you to go to Hell any more than you do.

In a way, it is a somewhat noble cause to wish to save someone from the fist of Hell. Misguided, but somewhat noble. However noble it these intentions are, the theology that states that if someone doesn't confess that Jesus Christ is their personal savior, they will spend eternity separated from God in a place of endless pain and violence is hurting all of us. If God is to be thought of as a parent, then this particular theology paints God to be an abusive parent. This theology says that there is something you can do to be separated from God, that there are conditions to Love.

This theology also takes away our power to actually choose God, to choose into Love. Telling someone to profess an absolute belief or else they are going to Hell is akin to asking someone if you love them while holding them at gunpoint. That's not a free choice to be in Love, to choose God. That's doing something under duress. Because everyone told us that this was normal, we developed a sort of Stockholm Syndrome, falling for our captors and vehemently defending them with every ounce of our being.

Evangelicalism, predicated on certainty, cannot entertain the question of Hell existing in any way other than eternal conscious torment because their power depends on it. I'd wager that they are just as scared as we are, asking the same question.

"What if we're wrong?"

...

Can I tell you a secret? I'm really over the word "deconstruction." I know it's an operative word and right now, it's the word that best fits what is going on for many people. I do wonder, though, would "demolition" be a better word? Aat least for me it's perfect, because my faith was stable for a long, long time until it just wasn't. The moment I pulled the card labeled "homosexuality" from my faith, the entire house of cards I had built for myself and protected over my lifetime came crashing down.

That's what I feared. Sure, I was slowly becoming okay with being a big ole gay, but the fear was, "If I'm wrong about this, what else could I be wrong about?" That's a conservatives' biggest fear, too. If they admit they are wrong about this, if they concede that progressive theologians have any sort of wisdom or something constructive to offer the conversation on faith, then it legitimizes our movement and takes away the power they still are desperately trying to maintain. There is a fear of being wrong that holds them back from meaningful dialogue. That is the reason they demonize so often. If they can paint themselves as separate from the rest of the world, they do not have to have compassion for the world or the suffering they cause in it. 'Cause they're just doing what they believe God wants them to do.

It is that lack of compassion that I find so surprising and so saddening. The inability to see the suffering of other humans, in fact, dehumanizes them as well. It's no small wonder they have such an issue with giving Love because they are unaware of how much Love has already given them.

I had another friend describe her faith transition as pulling on a string on the tapestry of her faith and life, and all of a sudden, it was just threads and threads of tangled mess on the ground. She just couldn't stop asking the question, and it wrecked her faith entirely. But what I reminded her was that now that she teased out everything and came to the glorious conclusion of, "I just don't know about anything anymore," is that now she got to weave together a faith that actually looks more like her lived experience of the Divine and less like white dude-bro Jesus.

What's interesting is that I was having this same conversation just a few weeks earlier. This particular night, my roommate Jon, as beautiful as he is goofy, came home to the sight of me prostrate on the floor of our living room. My childhood Bible was open in front of me, and then there was me, trying to read it and love it because that's what good Christians did. Even as a now openly gay Christian, I felt like it was more important than ever to spend time reading my Bible so that I knew how to defend myself.

But I just didn't know how to anymore. I had no idea how to defend any of this shit because... well, we made it up! *All of this faith stuff*, I said, *we just made it up*. I had deconstructed my theology of human sexuality. Within that, I had to deconstruct what the Bible actually was, what Jesus probably believed himself within his own context, and even further back. Black Liberation Theology would see the crucifixion, not as a substitutionary atonement for my sin, but as an act of solidarity with every bit of human suffering that ever was, was now, and ever would be. This was far more compelling to me than the narrative that I was a bad person and so God had to kill His Son specifically for me.

Think about what's happening in the mind of a child when you tell them that. "You are a sinful, horrible, depraved person, and because of that, God had to kill Jesus on the cross." That is awful. I grew up thinking I was *personally* responsible for the execution of Jesus. Every time I sinned, I felt my hand driving the nail into Jesus' wrist, a la *Passion of the Christ*. Now imagine that kind of responsibility heaped on top of you when you're also queer, and you can't ever stop sinning because your teen body is raging hormones, and everything that moves is an object of lust.

It's a wonder at all that I'm as well adjusted as I am. I look at some of my peers and can see how present this fear still is.

If fear is the fruit of a theological teaching, and if we also in the same breath believe that perfect love drives out all fear, then it can be argued that this theological teaching no longer serves us. Not to mention, the question of whether Hell is an actual conscious place you go when we die has been hotly contested for a long while. I, along with the French philosopher Jean-Paul Sartre, would say that Hell is real, but not in the way we think.

Hell, Sartre would say, is just other people.

But before we do theology around this, let's discuss what our spiritual ancestors believed about the afterlife.

...

The ancient world was, by and large, viewed in three separate areas. The heavens where the gods dwelt, the earth where we live, and the underworld where the dead await whatever comes next. It was what ancient people used to make sense of their experiences and to give some peace to the unanswerable question of
what *actually* happens when the soul leaves the body.

The modern understanding of Hell, especially the Christian version of it, has been influenced by both Jewish and Greek thought. However, if we jump back to the earliest versions of the Hebrew Bible, before God had given the law to Moses and Jewish religion was codified, there are writings of a place called Sheol. Father Abraham would have understood this place as the place where all souls go after death, regardless of the life the person lived. It's not clear what it was like, whether souls were conscious, sentient beings, or if it was just more of a place where the soul rested. This was before Jewish or Christian ideas around Hell came about. By the 6th century BCE, Sheol was thought to be a place where all souls awaited their bodily resurrection.

Can we just stop there for a second? Because this is huge. This is an example of a time when our spiritual ancestors believed something different than we do today. That is huge because it sets a precedent for us to argue for a different perspective, something many of us have not been able to do because of our upbringing. Growing up, I thought that everyone just believed the same thing and had always believed the same thing because no one actually cared to crack open a history book in my world. My questions and curiosity were stamped out because uniformity of thought is necessary for a power structure to maintain the status quo. To liberate ourselves, we have to get curious again.

Actual theories and understandings of an afterlife began to take after the destruction of the first temple in 586 BCE. Several of the prophets started speaking about the way God was going to redeem them beyond how they had been hurt. They talked about how God would restore their people. However, after 70 BCE, after the destruction of the second temple, the nation of Israel was theologically and socially wrecked. What did it mean that their God, the one true God, allowed for the destruction of His temple? What did it mean that the favored people of God were being exiled all over the Roman Empire? Was God not loving? Did God not care? Was God not powerful? For Jews of this era, the temple was the symbol of God's delight and favor. And it was gone.

In the past, it was easy for prophets to point at the collective sin of the nation of Israel as the reason for which God took his favor from the people. But what about the suffering of good people? Good honest people who sought to honor God with their whole person, why were they made to suffer as the unrighteous did?

This gave rise to the idea of Olam Ha Ba, or the world to come. In the world to come, those who suffered in this life would be rewarded. Some rabbis would use the term, Gan Eden, referring to the Garden of Eden in Genesis, to describe the blissful state that we return to after we leave this life. In this Gan Eden, only the truly righteous would be allowed. The rest of us average Joes who are just trying to be a good people would go to a place known as Gehinnom, and later Gehenna, for purification before entering into our reward. This name is taken from the valley just south of Israel in the land of Canaan, where the people of that land would perform child sacrifices. The spiritual place of Gehinnom was thought by some to be a place of weeping and gnashing of teeth, fire and brimstone. For others, it was merely a place where one reviews their life and repents of their past deeds before entering Olam Ha Ba.

At the same time, Greek influences impacted Jewish ideas of the afterlife. The concept of Hades existed in ways similar to Gehinnom, with the addition of Tartarus, an even deeper level of spiritual imprisonment in the afterlife. During Jesus' teaching, he refers to Gehenna, evil people being kept from the Kingdom of God, and also that the gates of Hades would not overcome the Kingdom of God.

Notice what Jesus doing here: He is mixing religious traditions, doing theology in real-time. That's important to note.

Fast forward to Medieval Christianity: some theologians were arguing that all souls, evil and good, and even Satan, would be reconciled unto God in the world to come. Some thought that Hell was the state, much like Gehinnom, in which souls would pass through for purification or simply be annihilated altogether. Other theologians at the time argued Hell was not a temporary stop, but the eternal punishment for those who rebel against God, even after the resurrection of the body. This teaching became the prevalent teaching throughout Christianity. As Christianity rose to power through the Holy

51

Roman Empire, it became a dominating thought throughout the world, with one of the most notable imaginations of Hell being Dante's epic poem, *The Divine Comedy*. The epic describes a journey into the underworld, wherein several circles of Hell are described to punish people according to their sins in life.

With all that in mind, we now must ask ourselves, what do we believe about this? Better yet, why do we believe it? Even better than that, what do these teachings do for us? Are they helpful in living well? If these differing opinions and evolutions in thought tell us anything about what happens when we die, it's this:

We have no fucking clue.

...

It took me twelve years to come to terms with the fact that my sexuality was not going to be changing by sheer force of will. I could no more turn off my attractions toward men than I could peel my own skin off. (So yes, definitely possible, but impossibly painful.) But once I accepted it, I felt free. I felt like I was no longer performing for God. I really felt like, for the first time in my life, the joy of being a true child of God because I could be my true self.

For me, I had to study a particular Biblical hermeneutic to see the Bible from a place primacy, undoing it verse by verse and objection by objection. This tool for loosening my mind around this one particular area then lead me to deconstruct all the other areas of my life. Honestly, I thank God I'm queer. Because if I didn't have to excavate my beliefs because of this thing that made me different, I don't know if I'd have been able to see the weight of oppression on anyone else as easily.

What I didn't know, like many of us I'm sure, was that beginning to question what you believe begins to open doors that lead to more doors. Questions lead to more questions. Doubt leads to more doubt where there never was any before. Answers do not satisfy any longer.

For me, my line of questioning went something like, "Well, if I don't believe in Hell, then what did I get saved from? And if there was nothing to save me from, then what was the point of Jesus? Also, what if Jesus didn't *literally* come back from the dead? If that's not true, then was he not the *literal* son of God? Is there a God at all? What if there isn't? Then what's the point of any of this? What if we are all just here by some happy accident and we've only got a few more billion years before the sun expands and encapsulates the earth? If humans don't achieve interstellar travel, the entirety of our species and all the rich history and culture will be lost to the cosmos forever. And no one will mourn us..."

This is where my mind went and still goes from time to time: existential dread. A great unknowing wherein I feel myself standing as a speck on a giant dirt clod, spinning through space at a speed that my brain could not comprehend. If hell wasn't real, Heaven probably wasn't real either. And no one can prove it either way, so why have we been doing all this religion shit? Why have we killed each other for thousands of years because we called God by different names?

I was heartbroken. The Jesus I knew had died (again), and I wasn't sure if He would come back this time.

A day or so later, I called my sister, Emmy. She's a queer pastor, and if anyone had walked through the doubt, I knew it was her. I told her that I didn't know if I believed in Hell or if Jesus was divine or if I was even a Christian anymore. I cried hot tears while I heard her silently holding space for me on the other end of the phone.

"Babe," she said, tenderly the way a big sister does, "I don't have an answer for you. But I can say that it's okay. I know plenty of good pastors who don't believe that Jesus was divine. I know plenty of horrible pastors who do. Is it really that important if you know for certain?"

It wasn't. There was a lot I didn't know. There's a lot I could never understand, like if there was a literal resurrection of Jesus' body or if there was a literal gay lake of fire in the great beyond. If I can never know, then...what? What does one do with an unanswerable question?

We start imagining what might be possible. After all, God's a creator, and we were created in Her image. Why shouldn't we get creative with this question?

...

What I find so fascinating about my initial inability to let go of Hell is that it didn't do anything good for me. Because wasn't it the fear of Hell that kept me bound up in fear of my sexuality? Wasn't it fear of Hell that kept me from experiencing joy and pleasure? Wasn't it a fear of Hell that told me it was better for me to die than to keep letting my body sin?

What does this do for me? Nothing. Nothing good, at least.

If this does nothing good for me, then why am I clinging so desperately to it? Why do I want to hold on to this?

Because it's an answer. We hold onto that which gives the feeling of a solid footing. But when we are intellectually honest and come to the reality that we can never know what happens after death, we realize that the solid foundation was only quicksand. By that time, we're so stuck in fear of God being angry enough with us to send us to Hell that we dare not question it. The longer we've been in it, the harder it is for us to unlearn a hardwired pattern of fearful responses.

That's why, even after we've left spaces that were abusive to us, we still ask that question, "What if I'm wrong?" And what if you are wrong? What would that mean for you? I asked that to one of my clients, and they said, "Well, it means that I'm fucking up right now. It means that I'm probably going to Hell 'cause I am not going back to that shitty church."

"And do you think you are wrong?" I asked.

They paused.

"No, I don't think so..."

So many of us feel the same way. We're all scared shitless that we are wrong and aren't saying anything. We put on a brave face because if we say we're afraid, that means we don't believe. In our mind, unbelief is akin to sin, and sin is not okay. It's that fear response that we have hardwired in our brain. But what has this done for us? What has holding onto this question done for us?

I think it's paralyzed us, and kept us from actually healing. We leave the abusive places, but the abuse lingers in our bodies. The spiritual scars keep our perspectives rooted in fear. We were taught our entire lives to squash our doubts and continued this practice far longer than necessary. Naming our fears as they are allows us to meet the part of ourselves that is still wounded and afraid with radical self-compassion.

The thing is you could totally be wrong. About all of it. We all could. But the equal and opposite could be true.

They could be wrong. About all of it. They all could be wrong.
There's a better question we can ask here, and it's this.
"What if I'm right?"

And what if you are right?
What if God really is Love?
What if God didn't just love you but actually liked you?
What if your sexuality is good and your gender is valid?
What if God doesn't hate you at all and celebrates every part of you that you can't stand?
What if God really does have a plan to prosper you?
What if God wants you to be happy and experience the fullness of life?
What if it really was all that simple?

My love, can I tell you something?
It is.

...

The number one comment I get online from folks is "repent so you don't go to Hell." People are very concerned about my soul, it seems. Again, that's sweet but misguided. But repenting because you will go to Heaven later isn't actually repentance. That's an exchange of goods for services. If we are being honest, the majority of western Christianity isn't even concerned near as much about cultural repentance as they are about individual salvation, which isn't Biblical either.

In the minds of Jewish prophets, when they talked about the salvation of Israel, it meant liberation for everyone in real-time. It meant having the boot lifted from their neck. It meant getting moving out of the Hell that they were living in. It didn't have anything to do with an individual saying a prayer or performing a ritual. It was a collective movement.

God was telling Israel over and over again that it wasn't about the religious spectacle of religion. It wasn't performing the act of worship that was pleasing to God. It was a transformation of the heart from fear to Love. The prophets were constantly reminding their people of this.

"When you come to appear before me,

who has asked this of you,
  this trampling of my courts?
Stop bringing meaningless offerings!
    Your incense is detestable to me.
New Moons, Sabbaths and convocations--
    I cannot bear your worthless assemblies.
Your New Moon feasts and your appointed festivals
    I hate with all my being.
They have become a burden to me;
    I am weary of bearing them.
When you spread out your hands in prayer,
    I hide my eyes from you;
  even when you offer many prayers,
    I am not listening.
Your hands are full of blood!
Wash and make yourselves clean.
    Take your evil deeds out of my sight;
    stop doing wrong.
Learn to do right; seek justice.
    Defend the oppressed.
  Take up the cause of the fatherless;
    plead the case of the widow."
–Isaiah 1:11-17 NRSV (emphasis mine)

When I hear people tell me to repent so I don't go to Hell, I want to yell back at them, "Repent! Because you are the one putting me there!" It is wild that people can hear that what they are doing hurts people, deny it, and continue to do the same things over and
over again.

I think about the work of Exodus International that wrecked and destroyed the lives of countless LGBTQ people, promising hope for change and healing from their homosexuality only to push them deeper into self-hate. I think about Bethel Church's Changed Movement, a group of promoting a form of reparative therapy to "heal" people of their God-given desires, telling folks that God loves them and wants the best for them and that God's best for them is denying their God-given attractions.

I think about sitting in my church growing up, when I was striving so profoundly to change my orientation to make myself pleasing to God, fasting days on end, praying endlessly, isolating myself because I couldn't trust myself not to be attracted to a person of my gender. Every time my eye would fall on an attractive form that it ought not to, I said, "Kevin, that's disgusting.

God hates that. Do not do what God hates."

My mind was a prison for me, a living hell where I was always dancing along the border of sinner and saint, Heaven and Hell. One misstep and I knew Satan himself would show up and drag me into the darkness. I was so afraid of being consumed by my desire that I learned to hate it. I would say shitty things about queer folks, and how they were not genuinely faithful Christians. I would say how much God loved them, but that righteousness had a price, a debt we owed to a loving savior who died for our wickedness.

I cried at every single worship service. I cried because I was so ashamed that I couldn't stop my feelings. And if I could just open up my heart wider, maybe then God would pour out healing. If I just stayed in the Presence long enough, perhaps I could touch the hem of His garment and be restored.

Sunday after Sunday.
Meeting after meeting.
Year after year.

God, why won't you fix me? I've done everything you've asked. Why won't you just do what you promised? Why won't you deliver me from evil?

I was living in Hell. Every single day, burning in the fire of my own shame. Each day, trying just not to fuck up. Each day, I worried that at any moment, God would strike me down. Most of the time, I felt desperate enough to die.

That verse from Isaiah strikes me. "When you appear before me, who has asked this of you, this trampling of my courts?" The tradition in my early twenties, when I was deep in my shame, was hyper expressive, quite charismatic, and had a lot of emotional outpouring during worship. It was taught that if we really go in, if I was unashamed before God, and danced before Him, my faith would be stronger. If my faith was strong enough, anything could happen.

Miracles. I was promised again and again that God would work a miracle in me.

Now I hear the voice of God asking me, "Who asked this of you?" Was it God, or was it my tradition? Was it the Holy Spirit or a spirit of fear? Was it Jesus, or was it my ego desperately needing to belong and being afraid of losing God?

I think we both know the answer now.

Now, on the far side of things, I see these words, and I think of the Church. I think of all the ministries created in good faith that tell queer folks that God doesn't love them as they are, and how many people take their lives because of it. I think of the kids who message me on social media, telling me their parents beat them when they told them they were queer. I think of the trans women of color who are being murdered in public, and no one is talking about it.

Your hands are full of blood.

There is repentance to be done, but it's not for being queer.

The Greek word for repentance is *metanoia*, and scholars would say that the closest translation would actually say it means "to change one's mind." That is what God is asking of us. Change your mind for the forgiveness of your sins. Change your minds because your thoughts lead to your actions, and your actions are killing people. Change your minds about those who are suffering. Change your mind.

Stop acting like you are so perfect, untouchable, all-knowing. Stop ignoring the cries of the people. Stop hurting people. "Stop doing wrong. Learn to do what is right; seek justice. Defend the oppressed."

It's right there, people. The Bible seems pretty "clear" about that.
If only all Christians took the Bible as seriously as we do.

...

Let's wrap this up, shall we?

"But what if I'm wrong?" That's still the question some of my people can't seem to shake.

What if I'm wrong about sexuality?
What if I'm wrong about Hell?
What if I'm wrong about this inclusive nature of God, and I'm just giving in to my sin?
What if they are right?
What if my pastors and my parents and my church and conservative friends are right about this whole thing, and I'm just being deceived by the devil?

And what if you are wrong? What if everything in this book is a crock of shit? What if I am leading you astray right now? What would you do?

Better question: how can you know for sure?
Short answer: You can't.

We can't know if there's life after death any more than we can claim to know what "God thinks about" anything, precisely because there is no data to measure. Now, this could lead you into a whole existential spiral, which is kind of healthy to have at least one time in your life, in my opinion. However, let's go back to the question from before.

What if you're right?

What if you're right about sexuality?
What if you're right about Hell?
What if you're right about this inclusive nature of God?
What if they are wrong?

What if your pastors, your parents, your church and your conservative friends are wrong about this whole thing, and they are just being deceived by the devil? (Even though you might not believe in a literal devil figure anymore, what if?)

I cannot tell you for sure if you are right or wrong. I can only tell you what I have experienced in my journey of following Jesus. I can only share the stories of my queer and affirming faith communities and point to the fruit of our lives.

Being able to affirm my sexuality the way God already did saved my life. I went from wanting to die to being desperate to live. My spiritual life has flourished. I've done more ministry as an out and proud queer person of faith than I ever did as a wannabe straight worship pastor.

I've become more honest. I'm learning to ask for what I want and know that it's okay. I'm closer to my family. My friendships are richer. My community is fierce and vibrant. I've been able to pay my bills and go to school and study something I'm passionate about. I go to an incredible church filled with people just as passionate about God's love and inclusion as I am. I have the privilege of going to conferences and meetups and events with other LGBTQ people of faith and drink deeply of their wisdom and love for me.

My life has only gotten better since I chose to follow Jesus out of the closet and out of those environments that would stop me from becoming all of who I am.

That's another thing: this movement is growing, and that's data we need to pay attention to. Was it not Jesus who told us that the Gates of Hades would not overcome the Kingdom of God? If I am to believe Jesus, that would mean that anything that is not of God cannot stop the movement of the Spirit.

Exodus International, the most massive ex-gay movement in the world, promising "hope for change" for thousands of queer folks and doing irreparable damage to many, closed its doors in 2012, citing that 99.9% of folks who came through that program didn't experience change. As someone who survived the practices of this organization, I can say that it made my life a living hell.

It made so many people's lives a living hell. Each day, struggling not to have "unclean" thoughts and working to push away any longings for intimacy and connection. All for the kingdom. Then they closed their doors because they saw the suffering they were causing. In my estimation, that is the Gates of Hell unable to overcome the Kingdom of God present in the resilience of queer people.

The mystics would tell us that God can never be known, only experienced. Believe me when I tell you that I've experienced God out here in this wilderness of faith, in the spaces where I've felt unmoored and floating with more questions than answers. There is endless possibility in a faith that is still wrapped up in wonder, mystery, curiosity, and trust.

With that in mind, another question: do you want to go back to the old way of living? Do you want to go back to those spaces that you know hurt you? Do you want to go back to those small beliefs that kept you bound up for so long?

I'm going to assume (and hope) the answer is probably, "hell fuckin' no."

So, you think you're wrong?
I'll make another assumption that you'll say either, "No, I'm not." Or "I don't know."

So, if you don't know, why not live in such a way that brings you joy and pleasure and connection? Why not believe in a God who loves you as you are and wants to bring you into new life and life abundant? Why not believe with a faith that equips you both for the hard shit of life and also reminds you of the beauty that exists in this world?

Why believe in something horrible when you could believe in something wonderful? What good comes from believing that God would make you a certain way, queer and curious and loving, and then punish you for being exactly as you were created to be?

...

I want to leave you with a story I read about a wise teacher from the yogic tradition.

The master yogi Paramahansa Yogananda was dealing with an irate man who stated emphatically that all evil people should, and actually do, go to Hell. As the story goes, the yogi asked the man if he had any children. The angry man had a son, and the yogi asked him, "Does he have any bad habits?" The man told him that his son drank and sometimes came home really drunk. His son would make a mess of the house.

"Well then," Yogananda responded, "next time he comes home drunk, place his head in the oven, turn up the heat as high as you can, and make him stay there forever."

The man was taken aback and said he'd never do that. "I love my son! I couldn't do that."

"Then if you, even with your human frailties, love your son so much that you would never punish him so severely, then imagine how much more your Heavenly Father loves you and would never delight or stand for your suffering in this life or the next!"

Even on the most basic level, the idea that God would willfully allow separation or torture of the beloved makes very little sense. If a theology leads you into a place of great pain, then it's bad theology. Tear it down along with the rest of it. We can't prove we are right, but we never could prove we were right. Being right was never the point.

Being loved is.

So let us make the choice. What do we believe. What has it produced in us? What good or bad is it doing in our lives right now? Why not change your mind? Why not believe in a good theology over a bad one? Why not believe that you are Wonder, fully made, instead of a broken sinner with no hope but to always fall short? Why not live into abundant life rather than dying this continuous and painfully slow death? The choice seems pretty clear to me.

And "how simple is the choice is between two things so clearly unalike."[10]

---

[10] A Course in Miracles, T-26.III.7:4

5
YOU'RE GOOD, BRUH

So what is "sin?" I was talking to a podcast host recently who said that sin wasn't real, that it was shame that we put upon others or was given to us by others. And in the sense that sin is a noun, some cancer that rests in our spiritual bodies, then no, sin does not exist. However, as a verb, it is still very much a real thing. It can also be an incredibly liberating concept when we actually name the correct thing for what it is. But we don't like talking about sin.

This especially true in the cute little progressive circles we live in. For many, it feels like an antiquated concept and a way for conservative and oppressive religious systems to exact control over their people. It's a trigger. We hear sin and we automatically think about our sexual attractions, our gender presentations, how we do or do not measure up to some metric of "success." And there's no need to dismiss that it can be triggering. And yes, that is true, this has been a weapon that has killed many. We learned that there is an in and an out to the Kingdom of white Jesus. To be a Christian means that you do things and definitely don't do other things.

To jump back to an earlier example, many of us who grew up in conservative faith and home environments were told growing up that having sex before marriage was a sin. Furthermore, we were told that a sin is a sin is a sin, meaning that no matter what the sin was, be it murder or petty theft, your sin condemned you before God, and you better repent or else. This view of sin and God and redemption is, at best, unhelpful and, at worst, incredibly damaging.

Further compounding the shame of our sin is the belief that we are, in and of ourselves, sinful from our first breath. The doctrine of original sin which permeates much of western Christianity has been a cornerstone of the faith since the 16th century when the Catholic Church formalized it as doctrine during the Councils of Trent. We can thank our dear brother Augustine for going more fully in-depth on this.

They've called it original sin: the idea that because of the sin of Adam and Eve in the garden, we, their descendants, bear the weight of their sin and thus are corrupt from birth. This means we require a perfect Savior to take our place as a sacrifice so that the justice (or wrath if you go by the really old hymnals) of God would be satisfied we can be reunited with God.

That logic works perfectly if you buy into the idea that, at your core, you're completely rotten and irredeemable. But how can a baby be bad? A newborn baby who doesn't have autonomy or advanced cognitive function, which is entirely reliant upon parents to protect and feed and keep it alive, how can this child who has had no chance to do anything and is, indeed, incapable of doing much outside of crying and eating and shitting, be sinful?

"Well, God's ways are higher than our ways." That's a response I can hear some pastor giving me as to why this doctrine is the way it is. That's shallow and boring, in my opinion. Sure, God's ways are higher than our ways, but God also gave us wisdom and discernment. The epistles tell us to "test every spirit" to see if it's true. Why haven't we tested this one?

Much like our ideas about Hell, our ideas about sin and our base nature have evolved over the centuries. The belief we are at odds with God before we are born is untrue. The idea that we are sinful at our core, incapable of doing anything good on our own, has harmed too many people. It has taught us to be co-dependent on a system that keeps us spiritually caged. It has stifled our growth and independence.

This theology has killed our imagination. I think it's time we reimagine what we believe about sin and self.

...

I was taken to a Promise Keepers event when I was in seventh grade. Promise Keepers was this big Christian men's conference who wanted to help men stop being shitty. They had speakers who would help them to be good, strong, masculine, Christian men who were like King David, a man after God's own heart. Granted, they were ignoring the fact that King David was also a murderer and a rapist, but who isn't picking and choosing what they want to read from the Bible these days, ya know?

(Also, who the hell takes a thirteen-year-old boy to a conference for whole grown-ass adult men? Looking back on it, it was so weird, and I was literally the only kid my age there.)

I remember the men saying this one phrase over and over again. "I'm just a sinner saved by grace." They would harp on this. They'd say they were no good, that on their own, they were worthless. Fast forward to the advent of Twitter. This phrase is still found on the lips, fingertips, and on the bios of what many of us call Husband-Pastor-Father-Twitter. It's a mindset that not only makes our separation from love more real to us, it also excuses the poor behavior of people in power. I can't think of a time in the past three years where a megachurch pastor hasn't been ousted from his position for a "moral failure."

What they call morale failure, the rest of us call cheating on your wife while also keeping a façade as an exceptional Good Christian™, condemning sexual intercourse outside of a committed, monogamous, heterosexual marriage, and also posing yourself as a sports agent. But what do I know, right? I'm just an unrepentant homosexual who is unable to do any good outside of God anyways.

Evangelicalism taught many of us that we were no good, that our very core is sinful, and no matter what, we can't help but sin. We have to rely on the Holy Spirit to renew our minds so that we can overcome the urge to sin. We are taught to take everythought captive and make it obedient unto the Lord, and by the Lord I mean a very cisgender heterosexual angry war god patriarchal worldview.

Why did we learn from such a young age, why were we are taught that we are unique and good, and at the same time, told that we can't help but be awful and terrible because that's just the hand we were dealt, being born into a fallen world?

My earliest faith memories are me going over how bad I was. My prayer journals were filled with entries of how bad I felt, and bad that I couldn't stop doing the things I didn't want to do. I didn't want God to punish me for the thoughts I had about the guy in gym class, or my hot student teacher who I would go to for tutoring because I was craving any positive male attention. But also, at the same time, I thought, *well, if I can't help it, God will still forgive me… so if I'm gonna sin, might as well sin boldly!* Weird, right? In my mind I was negotiating what was acceptable sin, and what wasn't. How far could I go without going too far?

I was conditioned to automatically assume my default is to mess up and to act outside of our integrity. So are many other Christians. And this grace to understand that we are creatures trying to figure out who we are on this planet, trying to get what we want and need while also fearing for survival, yeah, we can should have grace for one another in that. The issue comes when those in power are given grace but no accountability. And that's not grace, that's privledge.

Every white male pastor or Christian leader that I have heard of having a #MeToo or a #ChurchToo moment, or even a reckoning with their racist work culture invariably posts something remorseful, and when presented with ways to begin reconciliation, they simply go away for a retreat with their other white male best friends who are also celebs and megachurch pastors, and come back to the world a changed man. And almost always they lose little to nothing.

What's interesting to me is that the sin of one pastors infidelity, while devastating for those involved, is a fruit of a much bigger problem we aren't addressing. What was the environment that caused a man who had the whole world in his hands to act outside of his own perceived integrity?

We fear messing up so much. We are afraid of a God who is ready to smite us at every corner, for every misstep. And the higher the pedestal you are placed upon, by yourself or by others, the more horrifying the fall from grace. The more perfected the mask, harder the face crack in the face of truth.

That megachurch pastor who cheated on his wife had a some legitimate need that wasn't being met. And because he lived in a world where he preached that sex is only good if it's between one man and one woman worked until it didn't for him. He had a desire for something more and he couldn't ask his partner for it, and a desire gone unnamed becomes an animal who will not be tamed.

It doesn't make it right, at all. I say that as someone who has cheated on a partner before. I understand why I did it now, and I wish I could go back and fix what I did. To be honest about what I wanted and let the other person decide if they wanted to stay or not. But I cannot. Nothing going forward can redeem hurting my partner. But the question is the same for me as it is for anyone else who does something outside of their perceived integrity.

What is the environment you are in which causes you to get your needs met by illegitimate means? Is it a church that demands you to be perfect, therefore, as your Father in heaven is perfect? And that perfection drives you to your own edge? Are you being pressured into being something or someone who you are not? Is that causing you to be separated from Love?

Anything that separates us or blocks our perception to Love's presence in everything and everyone is sin. Be it in word, thought, or deed done or left undone.

And we are hardwired to think that this block is our default. Separation, however, is not our natural state. Communion is.

...

As a child, I knew that sin was just lurking around every corner, and so I had to take captive every thought and make it obedient unto the Lord. Otherwise, the devil, who prowleth like a roaring lion, would come and devour my soul.

I was bad. I couldn't help it. It's just the way we all were in this fallen world. We are doomed to forever fall victim to our sin.

How incredibly traumatizing thing for a child to hear that no matter what you do, God sees you as disgusting and sinful. Unless you get right with (white) Jesus, say the prayer, act like we tell you, and then God's cool with you. Because that's just how it works.

From a theological perspective, I was taught that Eve fucked us all up. She was the one who got a little too snacky in the garden and decided to give in to her temptation and then tempt her husband. It was the fault of the woman, and thus the whole of humanity would suffer. But thank *God* for killing Jesus to save us from this woman's one act of indiscretion. We can all rest easy know that talking snakes don't have the last laugh, and maybe if we prayed the sinner's prayer just right, then perhaps hopefully we'll not burn in the gay lake of fire, right?

This shallow reading of the Genesis-creation myth paints Eve as this stupid girl who just couldn't keep her mitts off a shiny piece of fruit after being sweet-talked by a snake. And yes, it's a myth, not an actual historical account of what literally happened. We know this because of science. (We also know that snakes to not physically talk with words like humans do. Unless you're having a rad LSD trip or you're a cousin of Voldermort.)

And honestly, been there, done that. Who hasn't been sweet-talked by our serpantlike, wise-sounding ego to do the thing that might be fun but isn't exactly healthy? We've all been there. We've all acted outside of our integrity.

When people hear "original sin," they may pull out that verse in Romans, stating that "all have sinned and fallen short of the glory of God." And yes, absolutely right. We've all lived outside of our integrity and outside of who we were created to be. You don't need to be Christian to see that people do horrible things or to fight against injustice. And yes, we've all sinned, but we're not sinners saved by grace.

We are, as many of my Lutheran friends would put it, Saints who sometimes sin. We contain multitudes and somehow are both at the same time. But where I place my primary identity, how I perceive myself, I believe, makes all the difference with how I interact with the world.

As stated before, the doctrine of original sin did not gain prominence in Christendom until the Councils of Trent in the 16th century. But what did we believe before we believed in our inevitable badness?

Goodness.

The Genesis story, while not a historical account, gives us a stunning picture to see humanity as God sees us. If you look at the first chapter, God is rolling through creation and calling it good. Light's good, the Earth's good, the water's good, it's just good. Good work, God.

And then we get to humans. It says that God, got down in the dirt, in the Earth and fashioned a human out of it, the *a'dam*, which translates as groundling or earth dweller or human, not "man." Fun Bible fact: the word for Earth here is *a'damah*, the female Hebrew reflexive of *a'dam*.

So God, *Elohim*, who is male in conjugation, consorts with the *a'damah,* the feminine earth, Mother Earth, to bring for Life. That is what is hidden right below the text. A sexual encounter of Spirit and Matter, bringing forth us. Is that not just wild?

And *Elohim* looks at the creation of the human and says, "It is very good."

It's been pointed out so many times by so many other writers that the only time God says something is not good in this story is when he sees that the *a' dam* is alone.

But the a' dam is called very good.
Our humanity is called very good.
Our base identity, from the beginning, is very good.

For the past two-thousand years, both Jewish and Eastern Orthodox scholars alike have scratched their heads at Christians who beat the idea of original sin into their people because the concept of original sin, as derived from the Genesis story, is not in the text. Nowhere does it say, "And God pronounced them bad or sinful, saying *Only rely on Me, because you're gonna fuck it up otherwise.*"

Are there consequences for their disobedience? Of course. But I wouldn't even call what happened in that story "sin." I see it as an allegory for the journey many of us take from being children into being adults.

The text tells us that while Eve was out doing the hunter-gatherer thing, picking berries and fruits and all the other dope things God had made in the garden, she comes across the Tree of the Knowledge of Good and Evil, the one she's not supposed to touch.

The serpent tells Eve that she won't die, but she will become like God, knowing good from evil.

Is that what being like God means? Knowing good from evil? Being able to discern what gives life and what does not? (This also begs the question: did God create evil if there is knowledge of it? If up unto this point, there was just good stuff, how could evil exist if no one has sinned, unless it was created? If God created evil, then is God to blame for our propensity to sin? Great questions that we never get to wrestle with because, again, bad theology. Anyways...)

The text continues in chapter three. "When the woman saw that the fruit of the tree was good for food and pleasing to the eye, and also desirable for gaining wisdom, she took some and ate it. She also gave some to her husband, who was with her, and he ate it."

When I put myself in Eve's skin, I'm 99% sure I'd have done the same thing. If I'm out in the wilderness and there is something good for food, why wouldn't I want that? Not to mention, I'm a human, and humans can appreciate beauty. This fruit was beautiful, so again, why would I not want that? And then, wisdom! Eve desired wisdom. So do all of us. Who doesn't want wisdom?

Why did God keep knowledge and wisdom from us in the first place? Does that ever strike you as odd?

When I see myself as a Child of God and see God as Holy Parent, I imagine the prohibition against the Tree of Knowledge of Good and Evil was like a parent wanting to protect their child from the pain in the world. Parents tend to want to create for their child a perfect paradise to exist within, where no harm could befall them. Yet, at the same time, God created us for growth and with curiosity.

Perhaps the sin was not so much eating the fruit, but the belief that we could ever be separated from God.

After eating the fruit, both of the humans hide their nakedness from God, to which God asks, "Who told you that you were naked?"

Hear that voice like a parent to a child who was hiding. "Who told you that? Who said it was bad to be naked? Who said your body wasn't worthy of being seen?"

If we see this as a literal story, God is kind of an asshole. Seriously, what kind of dick of a parent puts the candy jar in plain sight and tells their kid, "Don't even think about eating the candy." What does a child want to do then? The same thing we'd all do. It's just like our predisposition with anything. When we try to stifle our thoughts and our desire, those thoughts and desires only intensify.

So, why would God even create a world in which we had the potential to fail? It makes no sense. And it makes no sense because… well it doesn't make sense. And we've been trying to make logic out of an idea that is fundamentally illogical.

That's why we can't read this text as a literal text because if we do, it makes God out to be the asshole dad who kicked their kids out of the house after they messed up one time. Even Jewish scholars don't see Genesis as a literal story, and let's not forget that Jesus was a Jew.

But the Genesis story doesn't have to be literal for it to be true. When we can take off the burden of proof from this story and see it for what actually is, which is poetry, we can see it the heart of God much more clearly. I don't believe God made the prohibition against eating from the Tree of Knowledge of Good and Evil because God was a dick and just wanted to horde wisdom for Themself. I think God was trying to protect us from what we eventually would discover anyways: our desire.

To want anything is to be human. The fact that we have desire beyond mere survival is something that sets us apart from many other creatures on this planet. Our desire is really, at our core, to grow and to know.

The fruit on that tree apparently was good for gaining wisdom. Perhaps God wanted to protect us from that because once one has wisdom, they are then responsible for that wisdom. Before that, Adam and Eve existed in bliss, contented in the reality of their union with God. The wisdom they gained about themselves, the desire they sought out to follow unto its end, satisfied them until the thought that to desire meant that there was a lack in themselves. That lack perhaps being something God never wanted them to feel.

Perhaps the garden is the metaphor for all of us. My friend Grayson Hester, a fellow queer theologian, gave me this idea: as children, we are blissfully unaware of the forces of good and evil in the world. And then we taste it. We gain wisdom either by choice or by circumstance. Sometimes both. After that, we act accordingly. We are aware of how vulnerable we are. We are aware of our bodies and feel shame about them because they are the source of our suffering. We equate suffering with sin, but that is not the case. Suffering, at least in a spiritual sense, is a byproduct of desiring anything to be other than what it is.

The text goes on to say that God then leads the humans out of the garden. God curses the woman with increased pains in childbearing and curses the man to toil and work the land for his food rather than living in a garden where it was provided. Again, reading that literally means God is an asshole dad.

When analyzed through the lens of myth and legend, rather than needing to literally prove anything, one might surmise that our spiritual ancestors were trying to make sense of why the world is the way it is. Why was it that women had pain during childbirth? Why is it that humans had to struggle with the Earth and the environment to bring forth food? Wrong question in my opinion.

The question could be summed up in the same question every culture has asked since we noticed our own pain: Why do we suffer?

Allegorically, I see this story as a journey we all must go on. We were born from perfection into a world where we will hunger for perfection, and realize it is nowhere to be found except within ourselves and with God. To eat of the tree is not to make oneself like God in the sense that we are all-powerful, but to simply know right from wrong, to distinguish good from evil. The issue becomes that, with such powerful words, in our egoic humanity, we assign these labels to things that maybe we ought not to.

We label one faith tradition as evil and our own as good. We name a political party as evil and our own as good. We name persons evil and label ourselves as good. We label suffering as evil and lack of suffering as good. But, as Father Richard Rohr put it, we must walk the path of great love and great suffering to see the false binaries of good and evil to which we've subscribed.

The Tree of Knowledge of Good and Evil is a symbol of exactly what it is named –the knowledge of what is truly good and what is evil. But our ego twists knowledge to its own devices. It creates the false division between us and others, and by extension, ourselves and God, our Spirit and the Holy Spirit, our body and God's body.

To walk the path of Jesus, to practice radical grace, is to love our enemies and love our selves. It is to look into the face of those who would curse us and see the Beloved Family. It is to look at our own reflection and see the wounds we still carry and how we perpetuate that violence. It is to learn to heal that we may not pass on our pain, but transform it. It is to finally take the knowledge of good and evil to its end. It's to recognize the light and shadow in everything and everyone.

It is to lovingly name our practices of hiding who we are as sinful, as that which separates us from God because it causes us to hide from others as sin. If we hide, how will our Light shine? If we are asleep, how will we stir the world from slumber? And what leads us out of our own personal shadow, what leads us from waking into sleeping is the recognition of where we have been. We must recognize what we've done that has allowed us to be separated from Love, and how we have allowed others, or systems to do it to us and others.

That sounds a lot like repentance, doesn't it? We'll get to that.

...

God said, "It is very good." This is our identity spoken over us. Before we have done anything or left anything undone, we are very good.

Why can't we just believe *that*?

This sentiment is echoed in the gospels when Jesus is baptized by his cousin John in the Jordan River. Upon coming up from the water, the text tells us that the clouds opened up and the Spirit of God descended on Jesus like a dove, and a loud voice from Heaven said, "This is my Son, in whom I am well pleased."

Before Jesus had even performed a miracle or spoken against the establishment, before He was the drunk who befriended sex workers, before He was called the King of the Jews, Jesus was a Son of God. His worth and identity were confirmed from the beginning, reaffirmed as He entered his ministry, and proven by the lives He changed and continues to inspire unto this day.

What if we could do the same? What if we could hear God speaking over us our inherent goodness instead of the prescription of "your doomed no matter what 'cause you're (allegorical) greatest grandparents were hungry one time?"

When I can remember the truth of who God says I am and trust that nothing can separate me from Love, I am more able to act within my integrity. When I can ground myself in Love, I can forgive myself and others more and find peace amid the hellscape that is often is our present reality. I can continue the work of justice because the source of my being and the ground of who I am is unshakable and unending.

Isn't that a better way to live? To live from Love rather than for Love? To remember that worth is already affirmed and good no matter what?

What would your life look like, feel like if you believed you were actually good?

What would you do and how would you act differently if you knew you were already in Love?

There are so many ways to interpret the story of Genesis, as many ways as people are reading it. The question that comes to mind then is which interpretations and which applications are serving the good of humanity. For two-thousand years, we conflated writings about the Bible for what is actually in the Bible. Between Augustine being influenced by the dualistic philosophies of Plato, being at odds with his own sexuality and demonizing the bodies and the feminine, we've got a huge amount of problematic doctrine that is largely uncontested. We've surrendered our autonomy and power to a system that taught us to do so. As womanist theologian, Emily Townes, said in interview, we learned "how to consent to our own abuse."

But just as we invested our power into a system of belief, we are allowed to divest our power from them. We get to take back the power for ourselves, take back the authority given to us by God, and interpret scripture into life praxes which make sense, are generative, and actually lead us to a more meaningful, more abundant life.

I mean, come on y'all! Jesus said we would do greater things than he would. And, apparently, Jesus came back from the dead. One might assume that was, like, somewhat tricky, right? That being the case, if we could do something bigger than defeating death, then reimagining scripture and faith is a minor act.

Our miracle might not be our bodies being resurrected in real-time, but perhaps it could be our minds, our hearts, and our spirits being set free in the present.

I heard that if you have the faith of a mustard seed, you could move a mountain. We don't need to do all that. We just need to move hearts.

All that to say, if you take nothing away from this chapter, consider this:

You can relax. You're good, bruh.

You, your desire, your identity, all of who you are, it is very good.

...

Now, just because I believe that our base nature is good does not mean that we are incapable of sin. Much of our progressive mindedness doesn't want to name anything as sin, seeing it as an outdated word with a ton of baggage attached to it. And it is, but as responsible adults and working theologians, we have to unpack said baggage.

Here's my working definition of sin that I borrow from my friend Britt Barron (who probably borrowed it from someone else):

Sin is action or inaction that disturbs shalom.

Shalom is the Hebrew word for peace, and one might continue on to say that it is the peace of all things, the peace that passes understanding, and the balance and harmony in the world. As free agents in the world, we have the power to affect things because we have desire. If our desire for something causes suffering, if it disturbs shalom, it is sin.

Rob Bell would say that sin is a helpful word because we need a word to describe the indescribable horrors that plague us. Because what is rape? What is sex trafficking? What is the murder of trans women of color? What are all these mass shootings? What is systematic racism and poverty? What are all these things, if not sin?

If we look once again to the Hebrew Scriptures, the prophets continuously name a nation as guilty of sin. They understood it to be a collective attitude and community practice which devalued certain humans and elevated others.

For example, it says the sin of Sodom was not men having sex with other men. It was the fact that the people of this city were overfed while others went hungry and unconcerned about the lowliest among them. Their collective sin is what led to their suffering. The prophet Ezekiel writes, "This was the guilt of your sister Sodom: she and her daughters had pride, excess of food, and prosperous ease, but did not aid the poor and needy. They were haughty, and did abominable things before me; therefore I removed them when I saw it."[11]

The people loved themselves, they had more than enough, *and* didn't help the poor and needy. They willingly held back when they knew they could've done something to stop the suffering of people around them, yet they chose to do nothing. That was what led them to their ruin.

There is a cost to greed. It's that those who are satisfied are not the ones paying the cost.

Additionally, the prophets are always calling Israel back to right living. They called their people to move away from practices that exploited others, away from their collective sin into salvation, which they also saw as a collective reality.

Salvation to ancient Israel was not a matter of your "*personal* faith and *personal* salvation from Hell through your *personal* Lord and Savior Jesus

---

[11] Ezekiel 16:49-50 NRSV

Christ. Amen," but instead, it was the collective salvation of the nation, which looked like liberation from oppression in real-time.

The problem here actually isn't the idea of sin, but rather what we name as sin. The church culture I grew up with was so concerned with what I now see was merely personal sin management. I was taught all the things not to do so I, personally, could be right with God. We never talked about it in terms of our collective sin, or the things we did wrong as a church or society. Because we were the Body of Christ, so how could God's Elect do wrong? We had the moral authority, of course.

But we were guilty.
We are guilty.

The sins of the Church are rooted in its diseased social imagination, couched in a white supremacist theology, allowing for the enslavement of black bodies, the genocide of native bodies, the suppression of women's bodies, the exploitation of poor bodies, and the destruction of queer bodies, and it is of these sins that we need to collectively repent.

The Church has historically failed to see its complicity in the systems that are bringing harm to the masses. We wonder why folks are leaving the church at such a rate, but the answer is staring us in the face: we have failed to repent.

And we must.
And we are.

It seems slow, and it is, but I do believe that there is a mass collective movement toward repentance. It happens when we recognize our individual complicity in systems of sin. It's a collective waking up that is happening in our collective consciousness. It's beginning to express itself through white people understanding systemic racism and what they can do to end it. It is expressing itself through Americans finally understanding the impact of colonialism, African slavery, and Native genocide. It is expressing itself through increased representation in media, art, and, now, in conversations surrounding faith.

This collective awakening is expressing itself through every single one of us recognizing that we were once guilty of many the sins we seek to root out and expose in others. We must not allow ourselves to be divided by the mere knowledge of what is good and evil, using it as another dividing line between who is in and who is out. Rather, we must remember the reality that every one of us is made in the image of a God of creation. God put Their own creative spirit into the universe, causing things to become and grow and evolve. God put change as the only constant in the universe. This means that we can change. We can all change. We can all repent. We can all change our minds.

We sin on an individual level any time we do something that disturbs the *shalom* in the world, anytime we do something that violates the autonomy of another human. These individual sins we commit, from casual racist microaggressions or the fact that we don't know if our clothes and food are ethically sourced, are mere symptoms of a more extensive system that both makes it notoriously easy to continue these patterns and incredibly challenging to divest from.

We all have individual work to grow and become and repent. I believe that work, and I believe that all good and practical spirituality, looks like dismantling the systems which disallow us from living into the holiness of our full humanity, the systems that keep marginalized identities on the margins.

That's what it means to bring Heaven to Earth.
That's what it means to change.

Our unique ability to change, to repent, to choose Love over fear on a moment to moment basis, is the greatest miracle of our human experience. And this miracle is a naturally occurring extension of our love for ourselves and for humanity. That is the miracle we need today, and this is the miracle I hope to bring forth in my own life. It is the miracle I hope you know is available to you. And the miracle is simply the recognition of what is already there:

God calls you good. Just accept it already. It's as simple as changing your mind.

...

INTERLUDE II
A POEM:
"I'M NERVOUS"

I'm nervous.
I'm nervous that I am not enough
and that I am too much
That the fire which drives me will consume me
That if I stumble, I will fall
That if I'm not perfect he won't call
I'm nervous because I feel small.

And when I think about forever and beyond
And how the universe just goes on and on
That there are stars that died eons ago
And how there are some folks who just make me
yawn.

I'm nervous because I'm loud
And I'm loud because I'm afraid I won't be heard.
I'm afraid of the silence.

That when there isn't a like or a new subscribe
When the noise in my mind starts to subside the
Thoughts in my head start to collide
At once, there's a fire explosion
While my anxiety keeps me frozen.
I want to do something, but I can't do anything because
I'm nervous

I'm Nervous

That I'm not enough
That I am too much

What is it to not have to fight?
I swear, I must've been born with my fists up.
What is it not to fear your own words?
Not to feel sparks on your tongue.
Not to constantly worry you'll set fire to your timeline
When you were just trying to be honest.
Not to feel nervous that you're not enough.
Not to feel nervous that you're too much.

I'm nervous about the future.
I'm nervous to go outside because
Anyone can buy an assault rifle and walk into a club.
In a world where black folks are killed
Yet it doesn't rub enough pocketbooks the wrong way
To get something like background checks passed.
And I sit here.
On my ass.
Feeling passive
Feeling massively pent up
And desperate and confused and motivated
To do something
And also, somehow, hopeful?

I'm nervous, but I am hopeful.

I used to be nervous that I would die
If I had to be honest
That I'd lose it is all
If I asked to be loved.
But I didn't when I was.
And I did when I asked if I was
Not enough if I was too much.

I'm nervous about my body.
I'm nervous what I can't remember.
And I'm sad about what I can.
I'm nervous to be touched
But I crave to be held
Because if you hold my body
I don't have to trust you with my heart.

I know how to hide nervous
I know how to play the part of
savior
   lover
     sage
      leader
    pastor
   comedian
survivor
I know how to be anything but
       Honest.

I'm nervous because I love you.
I'm nervous because you want me,
Even the parts of me I try to hide
The parts I want to change
Thought patterns wish I could rearrange.
I wish I felt normal.

I'm nervous because I know I am not enough.
I'm nervous because I know I am too much.
I'm nervous but that's okay.
I'm nervous and I'm brave.
I'm nervous and I love you.
I'm nervous and I'm still showing up.

I'm nervous
and
     I will tell you what else I am.
I am here.
I am not enough
I am too much.
I am mixed.
I am wild.
I am queer.
I am depressed.

I am ready.
I am loved.

And so are you.

6
NORMAL

The first time I realized that I was different, I was a child in a toy store. My family was on vacation, and we wandered into a toy store in some touristy town. Mom told my little brother and me that we could pick out something in a specific price range and let us wander the store. That's when I found it.

It was a small, vinyl backpack. All of my friends at school had one like it, and I was so jealous of them. Primary colors of red and blue and yellow. The best part about it was the strap. If you unzipped it, straight down the middle, you could wear it as a two-strap bag. But of course, I knew the cool thing to do was to one-strap it because that's what the 5th graders were doing. I came to my mother and presented my choice of item from the toy store. She looked dismayed as she bent down to speak to me.

"Kevin, this is something for girls. Don't you want something like what Ryan has?" I looked at my little brother, holding a set of toy cars. No, I didn't want something else. I wanted the vinyl backpack.

I felt like I was in trouble. Something I wanted was not okay. It was for a particular kind of person, someone who wasn't me. A girl. I wanted a girl thing, and that was bad because I was a boy.

My mother's intention was not to hurt me or make me feel ashamed. She was doing what every parent would want to do: spare their child the teasing of the mean kids at school. And they were teasing me. Being in the south, even if I didn't understand gender exactly, I quickly learned that there were divisions among us. Some things were normal and things that were not.

Me wanting a toy designed for girls was not normal.
I was not normal.
And because I was not normal, I didn't belong.

...

Dr. Cheryl Anderson told me as I was beginning my journey in exploring my "calling," exactly what I needed to hear. She told me I was going thru this thing called "deconstruction." But she didn't use that word. She said, "Kevin, you're experiencing an epistemological rupture." Now that is a million dollar phrase, and so much sexier than deconstruction. Because it's not a pick it apart bit by bit. For me, it was an explosion. Something deep inside me broke and I realized the system I lived under taught me that there was a specific way of living, and I realized I could never and would never fit into that image of perfection.

And that's because these images were made in colonial, patriarchal, and capitalist worldviews, all idols to be smashed.

Dr. Anderson has this incredible talk she gave where she drew on the prophetess and lesbian icon, Audre Lorde, apply her ideas of the *mythical norm* to the intersections of faith and sexuality.

Audre Lorde's mythical norm as the state of being in the world which society at large would consider to be acceptable and good. It is a statement of value, and is made up of the identities that have been centered, held up, and praised for their understood virtue and understood value. In our world, tattered and disrupted by colonialism and white supremacy, the mythical norm we've been handed, whether we know it or not, is a person who is white, cisgender, male, affluent, able-bodied.

It is so normal in fact that for most of my life, and even today, I actively benefit from this mythical norm. I have a beard so I am read as male. I have pale skin so I am read as white. But I'm genderfluid and I'm Mexican and Celtic in my background. That doesn't matter though unless I give myself some outward marker of my deviation from the norm.

All of this is the white, cisgender, heterosexual, capitalist patriarchy expressing itself in our everyday lives. No one goes unaffected. But maybe you don't know it exists. The mythical norm has become so normalized to us. It's the water we swim in, and we don't realize we are boiling to death in it until it is too late.

However, it's true reality is in name. It's mythical. It is an illusion. It is this *normative* standard that was created for us to aspire toward. Yet, it remains mythical because it is unattainable for so many of us because, physically, we cannot embody some or all of this projection of assumed human perfection. In fact, even those we perceive as embodying said perfection always fall short because white supremacy is an idol, and idols all demand a sacrifice.

This idol of normality and goodness is not the norm for so many of us, and yet we want it. We desire this thing because we think if we get it, it will make us whole, complete us, make us finally happy.

We try so hard to become this picture of idealized perfection because the Church has sanctified white Jesus who fits this description, forgetting that Jesus was first and foremost concerned with those who were marginalized by both empire and religion.

To be normal means to have power, or at least the illusion of power. It is to associate one's self and aspire to the mythical norm of whiteness the to continue living without conflict. Even though we could never ever measure up to what the mythical norm prescribes, we try our hardest because we've been convinced that to be normal means to be loved. We have invested our love into this illusion because it gives the promise of life everlasting to distract us from the pain of the life we currently inhabit.

This mythical norm is an idol so many worship. It is a representation of a desire fulfilled, knowing full well it could never truly complete us. We buy into the illusion because, honestly, it's a nice story. It's easier to exist like nothing is wrong rather than face the reality of our world. The pain it hands out is extraordinary.

Normalcy also denotes authority. It establishes itself as the de facto expert on everything, universalizing the human experience and asking everyone to play the same game and expect the same outcome. It tells us that this is the way it's always been, and we can't do it any other way. This is the way to God. Get in line or get out. Moreover, the mythical norm would say that this way of doing life, the existing systems as they are, is what God approves most of. When we examine our experience of this theology of the mythical norm, we can see how it causes pain in every aspect of society.

It is the work of we, the people who find ourselves outside of the mythical norm, to imagine what a new normal is, both socially and theologically. It is the work of the people to begin taking authority back from the systems and theologies that have harmed us. This may feel difficult, or even impossible, but everything feels difficult when you do it for the first time. I'd argue that the spiritual transformation we see in the present age is something we are all doing for the first time, so of course, it's difficult. But difficulty doesn't mean bad or wrong. It means we're cultivating something, and cultivation takes time.

It means growing pains as you shed old skin, as you break old habits so painful it feels like breaking bones. But it not bone to be broken, but a breath to be taken.

The work of cultivating new spirituality is not actually difficult at all. It is merely different. It is actively choosing to do something contrary to what we have assumed for so long to be our nature. But it's not hard to do.

To embrace a new way of talking about God is as simple as changing your mind.

It's time to take back your authority, beloved. It's time for you to look at your story, your experience, and your own intellect as a source of wisdom. It's time for you to stop looking at a system that wasn't built for you and doesn't want you and build something new. It's time that we stop being afraid of those who can no longer hurt us.

…

"Authority figures are really authority *figurines,* animated by the power you have attributed to them. Just as you have invested that power, you can withdraw it."[12] The Church has played the part of an authority figure, and we've seen it that way. We've seen what the Church has given to us as normal. And what have we seen? What is normal for the Church?

Normal is women being abused and the men who abused them not being held accountable.

Normal is children being abused and clergy covering it up.

Normal is LGBTQ people being told they are loved, and then when they seek to engage in the deeper life of a church, finding out that their sexuality or gender identity will be their barrier.

---

[12] Alan Coen, *A Course in Miracles Made Easy,* pg 24.

Normal is Christians voting for politicians who are more interested in the short-term profits of gun manufacturers and war profiteers than the safety of people.

Normal is an economic system that helps only those who fit the mythical norm.

Normal is policing women's bodies, commodifying and objectifying them while not actually caring about their humanity.

Normal is putting on a brave face when you are so scared.
Normal is saying you know all the answers when you really don't.
Normal is blind faith that disallows for your curiosity and growth.

If that's normal, I reject it. I reject the notion that to be a straight person is to be normal. I reject the idea that my credit score or how much money I (don't) have in my bank account dictates my worth or my belovedness. I reject the patterns that damper my questions and my doubts with platitudes.

But, the best part about all this, this notion of what we have seen as normal...

It's a myth. Meaning that, while it carries some power, it isn't real.

How then do we begin establishing a new normal?

We must distinguish between what is normal and what is normative. What is normal is something in the state it should be in as it actually is. What is normative is merely a shared collective understanding of what someone considers normal to be. But whose collective understanding are we working from? For this, we must think about what our theological concerns are.

In previous chapters, we went over John Wesley's quadrilateral; experience, reason, tradition, and scripture. The debate among scholars, theologians, and the heretic scum like myself, is what shape this quadrilateral actually takes. Is it a perfect square, with each side of it being of equal weight and importance? Is it a rectangle, or maybe some rhombus or parallelogram?

Much like our sexuality and gender, like the nature of the Spirit, I believe it can be fluid.

In a world where the mythical norm is king of our imagination, the theology that is considered to be normal and orthodox is most often theology written by and for the Eurocentric mindset (read: white folks in places of power). Most of what evangelicals see as "correct" theology has been primarily shaped by the white male theologians and thinkers. Don't get me wrong, I love Martin Luther, C.S. Lewis, Tozer, and Augustine and, though it pains me to admit, I even like some of the writings of our dear brother, John Calvin. Hell, let's throw the apostle Paul in there, too. Even he has some fantastic things to say about what it is to follow Jesus. There are a lot of really beautiful theologies and pictures of God we see in their writings.

Yet their theologies are incomplete.

I feel about most of these writers the way Lutheran pastor and writer, and friend, Rev. Emmy Kegler, thinks about the namesake of her tradition. These thought leaders were "very ahead of their time, and at the same time, bound by their time."

These writers are limited by their social locations. Because they are white, they can never know what it is to be black. Because they are all (presumed to be) straight, they can never know what it is to be queer. Because they are all men, they can never know what it is to be a woman. This may seem like a straightforward observation, but it is profound because it clearly identifies what they don't know. And that is also the thing we have been trained to constantly overlook.

When we do theology from only one perspective, we fail to see the vastness of who God is, making the Divine into the idolatrous image of the mythical norm. We make God into a white, cisgender, heterosexual, affluent, able-bodied male because that's what we see as normal, as holy, as good because that's what we've been trained to see as normal and holy and good, and trained to see everything else as a deviation from said holiness.

This extends into the Evangelical and conservative Christianity propensity to force their worldview upon the entire world, pitting the world, which they see as separate from themselves, against their god, and themselves against everything that would oppose their god. They'd like us to believe that their way of thinking is normal, including the idea that the Bible is inerrant and we've thought this for the past two thousand years. That is simply not true. The idea of the Biblicist, that the Bible is the divinely inspired and perfect word of God and therefore unquestionable, didn't take hold of larger Christian communities until the 19th century, likely in response to the Vatican passing a resolution of papal infallibility.

So no, we haven't "always believed" this shit. We haven't "always believed" a lot of things.

That being the case based on simple historical observation, why do we still hold these theologies up as untouchable and unchangeable and as unable to be interrogated?

Because we have been trained to not question.

We have not exercised our imagination, thus diminishing its capacity to perform, like a muscle that has atrophied. Therefore, it is the work of the people of God to begin to work that muscle again. We must be prophets of imagination, seeing the world as it should be and could be, not for all the things it is not. We must dare to see the path forward in the cosmos of color that it is, where small religion would have us see it very stark black and white.

Most of our western and Eurocentric theology has been born out of what Black theologian Willie J. Jennings would say is a diseased social imagination: social because we rarely ever have an independent thought that isn't impacted by our culture and circumstance, and diseased because it has been grossly deteriorated over the course of the 20th century. The work of spiritual and inner healing has everything to do with healing the imagination, in seeing things through the eyes of prophets.

I keep saying "prophets," and that's precisely what I mean, but to be clear, I do not mean a fortune teller or even someone who is trying to predict the future. To be a prophet or to be prophetic is to name something plainly for what it is. It is not to name the future, but rather the future that will happen should a cultural sin continue in the present.

Prophets look at the establishment, and where evil exists, they name it. They look at what is considered normal, see its immorality, and dare to say, "This should not be normal." In an age like ours, we must make the dichotomy between what is normal and what is normative. We need people to start saying, "This shit is not normal."

That's not to say the violence we face isn't woven into the fabric of our society. By that metric, it was normal to have Eric Garner's body dead in the street. By that metric, the erasure of Native Stories and culture is indeed normal. By that metric, the death of high school students at the hands of a man with a legally obtained assault rifle is routine.

But it does not have to be this way.

The Hebrew Bible is filled with prophets critiquing Israel for its behaviors, continually standing on the outside of the establishment and throwing rocks at the stained glass, so to speak. They gave clear pictures of how Israel's lack of concern for the poor and for the least among them would affect them in the long term. The same was true for Martin Luther. He was a prophet, naming what was happening. Since the establishment, which in Luther's case was the Catholic Church, didn't change, his followers began a new thing. The Catholic Church called him a heretic.

But "the only difference between a prophet in a heretic is time."[13] Yesterday's heretics have ended up being prophets and heralds of truth. Right now, reading these words about questioning every part of our faith may feel dirty or wrong or sinful or heretical. But I assure you, by critiquing the establishment we love so much, we can work on reforming it, or we can confidently begin a new thing.

In ten years, once we're done debating all this stupid shit, so many voices that are presently condemned will be held up as visionaries. By engaging our prophetic imagination, we enter the same work as the One we claim to follow.

Jesus himself was a prominent heretic during his time on Earth. His ministry was built around questioning the intersection of empire and religion. He saw it for the unholy partnership it was, one that was more interested in control and power. He preached about creating a shared life that cultivated the most good for the most people. This challenged folks on his own authority. He always told people, "You've heard it said, but I tell you..." His heresies amid his ancient Jewish context became the bedrock of our orthodoxy today.

What blows my mind is that so many conservative people call me a heretic, telling me I don't know what I'm talking about or that I'm biased. The thing is, I don't have a problem admitting that I am biased. So is everyone else. We carry an entire life's worth of biases, of what we consider to be normal. It is the work of doing new theology that asks us to "start somewhere and to grow, [with the] responsibility to examine what we think we know."[14]

Yes, it is hard to do this. Deconstruction, as many of us know, is a total mind-fuck because we've never had to imagine anything more than what we were handed. We were never required to think outside of our spiritual boxes

---

[13] Quote from Bishop Yvette Flunders, QCF Conf 2018
[14] Micky ScottBey Jones, *An Invitation to Brave Space*

until our spiritual survival depended on it. We used to understand God. Now we realize that even our construction of what we think is God couldn't be God because God is beyond our wildest imaginations. It's no wonder we have trouble figuring this shit out. We are unable to tear down the barriers that face us because our diseased social imagination has deteriorated our ability to imagine anything outside of the systems that we have inherited.

The connection to Christian theological imagination is direct: *because American Christian theology was formed from a faith that has its roots in colonialism and white supremacy, the theology that arises from it is already, at best, causing suffering at best and, a worst, dealing death.*

...

Let's bring this back around: what does this have to do with the Wesleyan Quadrilateral? Everything.

Culture assumes norms. Our lived context assumes norms. But norms according to who? Women? LGBTQ folks? Black people? Native and indigenous populations? Transgender folx?[15] Humans with disabilities? I'd wager for those of us who grew up in conservative faith traditions, quoting a woman as a source of theological was almost as rare as trusting yourself to know what's best for you.

When we talk of experience, we cannot universalize our experiences as the norm. When we think about reason, we must ask whether reason is established by Eurocentric ideals or if it includes voices from the margins. When we discuss scripture, we need to ask who is interpreting and if it's being used to empower people or to subjugate them. When we bring up tradition, we must look at the whole of the Christian story, including our two-thousand year history, in its fullness and not pick around the parts we wish didn't exist.

For the majority of my life, I was told that we had the answers. I was told that the "Bible is clear."

Clear to who?
Clear for who?

---

[15] "Folx" is a rendering of the word "folks" developed by trans and non-binary communities as a way to denote a group of gender diverse and queer folx, versus a group of presumed cishet folks.

It was clear to colonizers in 1617 that slavery was Biblically tenable. When they purchased and stole African people from their homes, forcing them outside of everything they'd ever known, they did so with the assurance of their doctrines. Because of the sin of Ham in the Old Testament, these white men could subjugate and demand labor out of Black bodies. Because Paul said that enslaved people should treat their masters with respect, they saw it as a clear indication of God's approval to continue their practices. If we are being frank, according to the mythical norm of their time, colonizers had a better theological argument to continue stealing Black people from their homes and enslaving them than those who would become abolitionists.

Abolitionists were the heretics who became prophets.

See what I'm getting at? When theology is created and curated by only cisgender, heterosexual, white men, we have an incomplete version of the gospel.

We must change our minds and include the multiplicity of present-day, prophetic voices who are crying out against the injustices that are so clearly wrong. This is not to say that white men have no place in the kin'dom or in the work of doing new theology. In fact, I see white men as integral in transforming the social imagination of other white men, who have been perched in the high tower of their privilege for too long and are the hardest to reach except by one of their own.

Kwok Pui Lan, an Asian postcolonial feminist theologian, says "A postcolonial feminist epistemological framework debunks any claims to the innate form of feminine knowing that is superior to or subversive of male knowing and finds it embarrassing that any romanticizing suggestions that women, by nature, are more caring and loving, or closer to God." This means we do not discount or dismiss the voices of our dear brothers because all are beloved Children of God. We are merely bringing in voices who have fought to be heard elsewhere.

Often times, when privilege is challenged, it feels to the person being challenged as if they are being erased. But in reality, they are simply being brought into a fuller community of faith. They become one with community, losing themselves in the body of Christ, realizing it fully includes them alongside their new family. No domination. Only communion.

...

The need to include new voices in public theological discourse is evident. What the Church has been doing since I've been alive is killing people. It is causing the suffering of too many people. I could care less about what is considered orthodox because people, my people, are dying.

There was a period that I was going to a non-affirming evangelical church here in Atlanta. That's a whole sob story you can go read on the internet, but one thing I remember from one of my one of my pastors at the time was this.

"If we push too hard, too fast, we'll scatter the flock. And unity is what is important."

He was talking about me pushing for LGBTQ inclusion and participation at our church. I had been a faithful member for a couple years. I had tried to lead a small group but was taken off leadership because, according to another pastor, it would mean the church leadership would be "making a statement that they are simply not ready to make."

What statement? The statement that *I* was worth fighting for? Worth including? It made no sense to me that my pastor could see the pain he was causing right in front of him. Yet, his dedication to the mythical norm, of maintaining a façade of peace while he broke the news to the sad Queer that they weren't important enough to even begin talking about this "issue", his obsession with holding onto an incomplete idea of unity caused him to act outside of what I believed was his integrity.

And it is not all surprising, is it? Why would he have fought for me? Nothing about this truly affected him. He had no reason to fight because it would continue to not affect him. In fact, it would affect him in an adverse way. His career as a house church pastor would have been threatened. His wife's budding worship career would be stymied by an unrepentant husband approving of faggots praying for people and what not.

He had no idea what it was to be Queer, or how it felt to be kept from something everyone else had access to for not other reason than who you fell in love with. And he wasn't close enough to me to really have his heart break. He said it broke his heart, and if that's the case it must be still broken because he never did the right thing. He held the line.

I resented that. Still do. At the time I wondered how long would I be made to wait? A few months? Six months? A year? Two years? I was given no guarantee or timeline because it didn't impact my pastor at all. He was a white, middle class, educated, cisgender male pastor. Why would he care about how this exclusionary act would impact the lives bodies of queer people? He had no context and wasn't engaged with people different enough from him that it caused him to change.

Anytime I inquired about a timeline, or when we would talk about this more, I was met with vague statements. I was told, "Well, we hope to have a more robust conversation about this with the elder board." Always a delay. Never the right time.

Hopefully soon.
Maybe.
Could be.

I got this run around for the better part of two years. Always a not yet. Always we'll get to it soon. Always a just hold on. And I kept asking when I could get a meeting. This was important. How long before it became a central conversation in the culture of our church? And I became impatient. I often wondered how long I should wait to be treated like everyone else in the church that I tithe at? Better question: how long *should* I wait?

Between my stubborn attitude and my trauma bonded feelings toward this church, I got it in my head that *I* had to remain there. I *had* to bear witness to my pain because other people had to know. I was sure they would change their minds. I would be like the Syrophonecian woman, begging for scraps from the master's table. I believed that if I shared my story, if people saw my life and how the Holy Spirit was working in my life, they'd change their minds. If people saw how bad theology was impacting someone in their midst, their hearts would break, and this mountain would move. They would accept me. They would love me.

I was told that God values unity among the body. It was never a theological principle taught from the pulpit, but it was in the culture. It was a loyalty thing. If you had a problem and no one else thought it was a problem, then it wasn't taken seriously. My pastor seemed to ignore the part of the Bible about, "if one part of the body suffers, the whole body suffers."

If I wasn't happy about something, if I wasn't experiencing the joy of the Lord, it must've been my fault because everyone else is doing just fine. The difference, however, was that everyone else could participate fully in the life of my church. Everyone was not experiencing blatant discrimination at the hands of church leadership that claimed countless times to love my queer friends and me.

What's horrible about this whole thing is I thought that this was *normal*. I thought it was normal to get dicked around by my pastors. I thought long-suffering without the promise of payoff was holiness and grace lived out. I essentially consented to my own abuse because I believed that it was the right thing to do. I saw myself as the one who would suffer so that maybe other people wouldn't. In the end, my efforts yielded nothing but heartbreak because there was never a convenient time for my pastors to do the right thing.

It will never be a convenient time to demand that someone respect you. It will never be convenient to upset the mythical norm.

The Rev. Dr. Martin Luther King, Jr., while white-washed as a demur and temperate civil rights leader who practiced non-violence and didn't demand too much of anyone, has much to say on the delay of justice:

> *For years now I have heard the word 'wait.' It rings in the ear of every Negro with piercing familiarity. This 'wait' has almost always meant 'never.' It has been a tranquilizing thalidomide, relieving the emotional stress for a moment, only to give birth to an ill-formed infant of frustration. We must come to see with the distinguished jurist of yesterday that "justice too long delayed is justice denied."[16]*

It is easy for people in places of power to fight to maintain normalcy because they've never felt the sting of rejection. They don't know people who died from complications from HIV. They aren't involved with queer community. They don't have many black friends. They don't know any Muslims. They don't know anyone who died from a bullet shot from a legally obtained assault rifle.

Even when we bear witness to our pain, those in power will do anything and everything to get around the fact that their attitudes, their inaction, and their theology is complicit in our suffering. They deny that those who suffer have anything to do with them because to do so would be to give up the illusion of being a "good person." It would be to awaken from the frightful dream they entertain ad nauseum in which they fear falling from grace.

King goes on to say later in the letter:

> *First, I must confess that over the last few years I have been gravely disappointed with the white moderate. I have almost reached the regrettable conclusion that the*

---

[16] Rev. Dr. Martin Luther King, Jr., *Letter from Birmingham Jail*

Negro's great stumbling block in the stride toward freedom is not the White Citizens Councilor or the Ku Klux Klanner but the white moderate who is more devoted to order than to justice; who prefers a negative peace which is the absence of tension to a positive peace which is the presence of justice; who constantly says, "I agree with you in the goal you seek, but I can't agree with your methods of direct action"; who paternalistically feels that he can set the timetable for another man's freedom; who lives by the myth of time; and who constantly advises the Negro to wait until a "more convenient season." Shallow understanding from people of goodwill is more frustrating than absolute misunderstanding from people of ill will. Lukewarm acceptance is much more bewildering than outright rejection.

Can I get a witness?

It's not the people in government positions who are the most significant barrier to liberation for marginalized folk. It is the nice, well-meaning, middle of the road, "I-don't-wanna-talk-politics-in-church" Christians who fail to un -derstand the suffering of those most affected by bad theology.

This behavior, of lukewarm attitudes on issues of justice, is the result of the assumption of normality. As modern-day followers of Jesus, the Holy Heretic and Prophet, those charged with doing greater things than that of Jesus, we have the authority to call out harmful, normative behaviors. We have the right to call out the bad theology where we see it and establish new norms for ourselves.

We get to decide. We get to join in the chorus of voices from thousands of years and ask questions and prod the scriptures, seeking the Word of God outside of the colonial and hegemonic understandings of the scriptures. We get to set the new normal.

...

Isn't that exciting?

Isn't that utterly terrifying?

We are in a season of embarking on a journey to explore the wild, unknown, mysterious, wonder of God.

Imagine, if you can, how free we will be when we can shed the shackles of the theological systems of that which is killing us. Imagine a sense of wild, awe-inspiring, wondrous Love, of God's presence in everything. Imagine being unmoored, floating the mystery that is Divinity and Hope. Imagine not needing to have answers. Imagine seeing yourself reflected in the pulpits of churches everywhere. Imagine a world in which the church is known for its social engagement and dedication to justice and mercy, marked by its humility.

Imagine all of that.

Now, try to imagine all of that as normal.
What if it was?
What if it could be?

I, as a person of hope and annoying optimism, imagine that it not only is possible. I imagine it is the will of Love.

7
THE CHAPTER ABOUT SEX

To say that I had a subpar sexual education would be an understatement. The entirety of my "talk" was my mother sitting my younger brother and me in the living room and uncomfortably explaining how the sex was supposed to work.

"I know you guys have had health class at school," she began. She didn't explain the mechanics of sexual intercourse concerning the penis entering the vagina, or where babies came from. She did, however, impress upon us that sex meant more to women than it did to men. For women, it was emotional and deeply personal. For men, it was merely "getting off." And that was the first and only time I heard my mother used the phrase "getting off."

"Do you know what I mean by that?" She asked. I had never heard that euphemism before, because, again, I had a subpar sexual education. She never really explained it, but after a little bit of stumbling through uncomfortable metaphors, I finally got it. She meant the moment of climax. She meant ejaculation. Why was it so hard for her to just say it out loud? Why was it so embarrassing?

I can't remember much else of what she said to us, but I do recall the conversation not lasting much longer than that. The main point I took away from that talk was don't have sex with a girl because if I were to break up with her, it would break her completely.

My internal response?
"No prob."

It was my third year of high school, and I was still intensely repressing my sexual orientation. I was trying to be as straight acting as possible, lest I become a target for the assholes at school. However hard I worked, though, trying to hide this flame under a bush only reinforced what I think was an open secret at my school. "Kevin's super gay, but he's also super Christian. Best not to ask."

What is interesting is that puberty shielded me from a lot of flack. My voice dropped, and I began growing hair on my face and chest (every other surface of my body), and this protected me in some ways from getting bullied. Jacob Tobia, in their book *Sissy*, reported a similar experience. It was almost as if being what was considered to be manly gave you a pass on the other stuff. But being manly didn't equate to attractiveness, however. Add to that the fact that my voice has a little bit of that lilt that gay guys are stereotyped with, and I was set up to be pretty chronically single for most of high school, with the occasional good Christian girlfriend here and there. But even though I was a good Christian boy who wasn't having sex, I still loved hearing about it.

The fascination was two-fold. On the one hand, I was a perfectly healthy, repressed, horny teen with so many hormones rushing around my body that I had no idea what to do or feel half the time. Hearing about my friend's sex lives gave that energy somewhere to go, almost like I could live vicariously through them. I would listen intently, wondering about how I could cultivate those same attractions.

One of my buddies from choir, who was ironically also on the football team, talked to me about him and his girlfriend's sex life often. I was enraptured and, to be quite frank, would wonder what it would be like to feel everything my friend was describing, but with me. It was one of those friendships where I secretly developed feelings for him and was always just a touch jealous of his girlfriend.

As soon as I would catch myself, I'd snap myself back to reality. I'd use the tools given to me:

Snap the rubber band around my wrist to feel a little bit of pain. I was taught to condition myself to associate the unwanted attractions with pain. Repeat until I can avoid them altogether, all the while hoping that God works some sex magic on me to make me not want to have sex with my best friends.

Ya know, typical teenage feels.

(What's funny about remembering this: I think the rubber band thing actually is what lead to the slight kink I have for a hard slap on the ass and a bit of biting in bed. I think I started associating pain with arousal, perhaps? I don't really know for sure, but for me, a little bit of pain goes a long way. So, shout out to my ex-gay therapy for making me kinkier, I guess.)

These feelings towards my guy friends caused me to develop a deep shame. Not for the part of wanting to be intimate, but because of *who* I wanted to be intimate with. I felt gross all the time. Despite being told that it was a sin like any other, I knew it wasn't. Couldn't be.

Because sin was death. Sin was the thing that separated us from God. Most importantly, sin was a conscious choice. It was the choice to do things that didn't align with God's heart for the world. I knew, I just knew, deep down, that I never chose to be attracted to other men.

So how could this be?

"We all have our struggles."
"God doesn't give us anything we can't overcome."
"He gives the biggest burdens to the strongest warriors."
"If Jesus can come back from the dead, Jesus can help you overcome your unwanted same-sex attractions."

It didn't matter why I was the way that I was. It only mattered that I did what my pastors told me, what my family expected of me, and what I thought God wanted. It was made clear to me that God didn't tolerate sins, and that when we lived outside of God's will for our lives, we lived outside of grace and protection.

I was afraid of asking questions because questioning church teaching also meant, by extension, to question God. To question something meant that you doubted. Doubt was not tolerated among the faithful.

"Abraham simply believed, and it was counted to him as righteousness," one of my mentors said, "You have to do the same."

Simply believe. Don't question. Don't ask why. Just know that we've figured it out.

And so, I tried. I tried doing the right thing, being the right kind of guy. I didn't have trouble with being too handsy with women, nor wanting to deflower a young maiden. I was *such* a good Christian. But despite my good behavior, despite my status as a "good Christian," I was always scared. I always felt gross, and still I desperately wanted to please God.

The most significant prayer I prayed was, "Why me, God? Why do *I* have to suffer with this?"

"Well," the voices of my ex-gay therapy told me, "Even Job suffered greatly, and yet he did not curse God. He was faithful, and we are called to do the same."

But even Job's suffering ended. Job got an answer from God. Yet we, the queer and faithful, we waited and wait and are still waiting on relief that will likely never come. We suffered nights on end of perceived distance between God and our bodies. We longed to be reunited and yet were told that this part of who we are, these feelings we could not help but have, kept us from Love.

There is nowhere in scriptures in any faith tradition that gives us an example of someone suffering unduly without reason for an undetermined length of time. To ask this of queer folks, to ask them to give up their sexual identity and any chance at cultivating deep intimacy and love for themselves is to ask us to consent to our own abuse. To ask this of queer folks is deeply unbiblical. To ask this, is frankly, so incredibly unkind.

...

I had this illusion, or fantasy, you might say, in my head when I started my coming out. I thought it'd just line up. I'd be handed the homosexual agenda, clearly labeled "GAY" in big, glittery, Lisa Frank inspired letters. I would be given a drink ticket, good for a vodka soda only. Finally, I'd be able to go on dates with good, Godly men who also wanted to save sex for marriage. I'd be married by twenty-six, a mere two years off my life-plan I set during my purity culture promise days, with two kids and a dog and an house dressed to the nines in West Elm.

I've been out for half a decade, and I'm still waiting for that agenda containing instructions on how to ruin marriage for the rest of these heteros.

The truth became clear to me very quickly after coming out: life out of the closet was nothing like it seemed. It was both worse than I thought and better than I thought, all at once. It truly exceeded my expectations in every direction.

Rather than an apartment, I shared a small room in a basement with my friend, Casey, who was also a missionary with me, and who for sure wasn't queer until he was. Rather than drink tickets, it was boxed wine. Rather than going on dates with good Godly men, I was becoming a serial make out artist because Lord knows I didn't put out on the first date. I was not a slut (yet).

Up unto this point, much of my theology was heavily influenced by what my colleagues would call the "Biblical case for LGBTQ inclusion." It was revolutionary in the way that I approached scripture. For the first time, I was reading it from my own perspective, along with the voices of women and trans folks and queer folks and people of color. I saw how liberation for queerness was tied up in the liberation of black and brown folks, in the liberation of immigrants.

The theology that led me to understand my own liberation was built upon the voices of so many spiritual ancestors who came before me. What these voices begged me to do, what Jesus was begging me to do, was go further.

The question for me and many of us on the other side of our epistemological ruptures is, "What do I believe about sex? And why do I believe it?" Is it really this thing that is dangerous and should only be used in the confines of a monogamous, heterosexual marriage between two equally yoked people? Or is it perhaps just a bit more complicated?

Furthermore, what do I believe about it in light of the tradition of my faith, the scripture I read, my reason given to me by God, and my own lived experience?

That last part was a little tricky for me. I was a good Christian boy who didn't have sex because I believed that sex was best had within covenant marriage. I didn't know why at all. I just knew that's what was acceptable. It was, unbeknownst to my own damn self, still based in the shame of my own attraction. I was carrying some internalized homophobia about wanting to have sex with a man. Perhaps if I got married, then it would make it okay. Maybe my family, my church, the world will see me as normal and acceptable.

This is respectability politics, in its most basic form; that is the belief that one must alter their appearance or performance of self to be considered credible or be taken seriously. It is to ascribe one's self to the mythical norm, to try and reach that level of perfection. And for a flamer like me, to tone down the rainbow is no easy feat.

(Sidebar: I do not pass as straight. Couldn't even if I tried. If I wore a certain kind of outfit, like camo or something, and didn't say anything, then maybe I'd pass as a straight person. But the moment I open my mouth and say anything in my natural voice, it's evident which team I play for. Which I don't hate. It is what it is. I'm pretty femme. I like it this way. I desire to be myself entirely in ways that make me feel comfortable and empowered. It is this desire, planted firmly at the core of my being, that allows me to move through the world with boldness.)

When desire is not trusted or given voice, when we learn to abhor our desire, we are then programmed to hate our desire and everything that goes with it. Why is that? It's because we don't see our attractions as normal.

Because our attractions don't look like that mythical norm.

Because our kind of relationship style isn't in the Bible.

Because I can't naturally make a kid if it's just me and another dude having sex.

Because of all of these things, I feel less than loved.

Because of all these things, I can never be normal, holy, or good.

That's where we have to go to. So many of us, queer and straight and everything in between, carry around this intense disdain for our desire. This doesn't just apply to sex, it refers to everything. We are creatures who want.

Part of my journey in discovering my own sexual practice came from destigmatizing my desire and unshaming the specific desire for sex.

Because really, at its core, our desire for sex is an extension of our desire for intimacy, to be known, and to experience pleasure. That doesn't seem like anything shameful, does it?

...

When I first started having sex, it was still ripe with shame. I continuously looped on the same scripts handed to me. I was told things like, "Sex between two unmarried people is like crumpling up the flower that God gave you. You leave part of yourself behind when you give yourself away to everyone. If you have gay sex, you're gonna get AIDS and die." Those kinds of messages kept me from straying too far. First it was just look at porn one time and then confess it and then it's over. And then it was maybe I can like make out with boy at a party but make sure that I never catch feelings because, eventually, God will bring me a wife.

But if you give a mouse a cookie, it's going to want some milk. Desire will find expression in one way or another, its needs being met by your conscious mind our by your unconscious action that you would call your sin nature. The desire for sex is so normal for the majority of humans, and most other mammals and reproducing creatures. The biological drive is to pass on our genetic materials, but as evolved creatures we also recognize that it feels really fucking good. It releases some delightful chemicals in the body that make us feel better, and it helps release stress. That's why masturbation is actually good for you, but we can cover that later.

I yo-yo'd in my walk with God when I struggled with same-sex attraction. I would be good for a long time, and then all of a sudden, out of seemingly no where I'd get this urge to masturbate. And then I'd tell my brain, *NO DON'T THINK ABOUT GAY SEX!*

What happens when you tell your brain not to think about a rainbow unicorn snorting gold cocaine off the arc of the covenant from Indiana Jones? You can perfectly visualize a rainbow unicorn snorting gold cocaine off the arc of the covenant, right?

I was constantly not thinking about sex by thinking about sex. So many of us were. (Or, we obsessed about marriage and how soon we could get married so that we could have sex.) And the mind is a powerful thing. And even though I told myself I didn't want that, my body was telling me something different.

In high school and even around my church circle, I had dated a few women. It felt like a great friendship, and I enjoyed making out, but the desire to ever take their clothes off mortified me. Not because boobs and vaginas are gross, but because I am genuinely not often turned on unless there is another penis involved in some capacity. And that data point, that I wanted to be intimate with another man, was terrifying.

It felt wrong. Why did I want it? Also, what was so bad about it? Could it really be as sinful and bad as they say it was? People had sex all the time, and they seemed fine… but I was a Christian so, I don't know…

Despite my fear, curiosity eventually led me to the dating apps, casually talking to strangers, seeing more flaccid dicks than I ever wanted to see, and letting the thrill of being desired flood the system. It felt thrilling and made me come alive a bit.

Eventually, flirting didn't do it for me anymore, so I took it to the next level. I invited a guy back to my room at a point when I was still deeply closeted. While out somewhere, speaking at a college, and staying in a quaint, cozy little B&B hotel situation, I got to feeling lonely, and moreover, bored. This town had nothing to do and no people to speak of besides the college, and being a graduated person among young twenty-somethings did not appeal to me.

I downloaded Grindr (a dating app known to be more of a hook-up app in the gay male community). Within moments my phone was buzzing with messages and unsolicited dick pics. It was overwhelming at first, but also so thrilling because, what if this actually happened? What if a guy came over and we had sex? And it was just no strings attached. I'd go back to my life as a good Christian when I got home. What was so wrong with this anyways?

I chatted up one guy in particular. He was an art professor at a local college. Instantly, my head filled with all the teacher/student porn I'd watched. I was being punished for not studying hard enough by making it hard *for* him. Very steamy.

Too much? Sorry about that. I'll reign it in.

A few messages later, I asked if he wanted to come over to my hotel room. We agreed to just oral: He said he'd be there in thirty.

This was really going to happen. I quickly stripped and hopped in the shower, styled my hair, and put on one of my jackets as if I was going to meet this guy out for a date. And then I waited.

Twenty minutes to go.

I generally knew what to do. At least I thought I did. He'll come in, and then I'll take off his clothes, and then he'll take off mine, and then we'll... lay down on the bed? And then... Like...

My body began to shake with the visceral realization that I actually had no idea what the fuck I was doing, in every sense of the phrase. I had no idea if he would be impressed or if he'd like what he saw. The only oral experience was this one time in college, but I didn't like it (because of past trauma that I had yet to uncover).

"Breathe," I told myself. "Breathe in and know you're okay. You're an adult. You can do this. Adults have sex all the time."

But I felt like a child. I felt small and scared and so nervous that my body was still shaking ten minutes later. I breathed. I focused. I slowed my heart rate, and finally, after feeling like it had passed, there is a knock on the door. I go to answer it.

"Hi," he says with a smile and a salt and pepper beard. He's shorter than I imagined, but I like it. He comes in, takes off my jacket. We kiss a little bit. He asks me about my tattoos, the Lion of Judah and the Lamb of God on my forearms. He had zero context for religion nor my evangelical upbringing, so my explanations were met with blank stares, and we decided to just skip over that.

"I've never done this before," I confessed. He looked confused. Not done what before? "I've never hooked up with a guy from an app before." He assured me it was okay. As he moved closer, my body began to shake again. My cheeks glow a bright red, and my breathing gets shallow.

"You know," he said lovingly, "You know we don't have to do this. Do you want to have sex?" I shake my head and just barely mouth a no. He nods, moves from the bed to the chair, and I apologize. I spill my whole life story to him that I was a Christian but was also attracted to men, and I didn't know what to do about it. He just listened. He looked at me with such pity and compassion and frustration.

"So many repressed queers," he trailed. Looking at me with his serene eyes, he asked, "Do you really think God would make you gay and then ask you to repress yourself for your entire life? Seems kinda fucked up, to me."

When you put it like that, it seemed really clear. *But... the Bible*, I felt my head say.

We talked for a few more minutes. I had never had an honest conversation with another queer person before. Not once confessed that I desperately wanted this to be okay. In fact, I think it was the very first moment that I was honest, period. This stranger knew me better than my closest brothers and sisters in Christ. This stranger was a safer place than the Church was. After a while, he put his jacket back on. Walking toward the door, he paused and looked at me sitting on the bed, with compassion that I've seen in very few other people.

"I hope you learn to love yourself, Kevin." He smiles sadly. I return the smile. Then he turns, opens the door. Click. He is gone.

I cried for a good long while after he left. For the first time, I knew what I had been missing. I felt the absence of closeness, of being seen, of being held. For the first time, I realized how much I was missing. I realized I yearned to have a voice, to sing my own song, and yet the voice of my body was being silenced. The power of being touched, the weight of another person's words telling you that another way is possible. This man's parting words became breadcrumbs for me to follow toward my own freedom.

How did he get there? How is that he was able to just stroll into a hotel room with such freedom, ready and wanting to have sex with a, and I was left shaking in my boots?

How was I going to get free of this? Something had to give.

...

That wasn't the first time I was intimate with another man. The first time was actually in college. My first boyfriend, we'll call him G, was my first real relationship. We met backstage at the Christmas concert during my undergrad. He played the violin and had an eyebrow ring. So edgy.

We came out to each other on video chat. We started dating before spending any meaningful time together because my anxious attachment style really loved to move at lightning speed.

During winter break, between semesters, he and I met in Richmond for a date. It was halfway between our homes in Virginia, and we knew we wouldn't run into anyone at this outdoor mall. I remember seeing him in the parking lot and rushing to him. When we kissed, it was like my whole body ignited in a way I had never felt before when I kissed a woman.

Fireworks. That's the best way I know how to describe it.

For once, I decided to trust that feeling. It felt so good to feel good. Spending most of your life hating yourself for wanting to be held by someone who might love you, and then to release yourself from that hate; it's like tasting honey and cinnamon in your oatmeal after eating it plain your whole life. It's wholesome.

It was, however, as many first relationships go, a flash in the pan. It burned hot and fast. Then he joined a frat and continued to become who he was meant to be. I knew it was over when the wine I was saving for our three-month anniversary ended up in his Nalgene bottle as he walked around campus, pre-gaming for a thirsty Thursday party.

At first, I saw our breakup as a punishment from God. It was proof-positive that gay relationships just didn't work. It was all based on sex and lust and wasn't good at all.

But that wasn't true. Sure, G and I had some serious issues, but we were also closeted to most of the world. We both had a ton of baggage around religion and sex. You can imagine how hard it is to enjoy getting a blow job when you're also worried about the Second Coming happening at any minute. (Not my joke, but still funny all the same.)

I see that relationship as something vital for me. It was the first time my body was felt good touch. It was the first time I let myself be naked with someone, both emotionally and physically. He was my first, "I love you." G was Christ to me for the time I had him. He showed me that another reality was possible. He allowed me to say yes to what my body was feeling, what my body was asking for. What was my body asking for?

To be free.

It took me a long time to remember how good that relationship was for me. Most of my life, I was told to trust my feelings, or my body, was to fall headlong into the sin of the flesh.

A friend of mine told me a story about when her and her wife kissed for the first time. She said it was the first time her body came alive. It was a feeling of '*Oh! This is what it is supposed to feel like, isn't it?*' Yet, she didn't trust it. Her love story ends beautifully. Still, the moments in-between that first kiss and the present day are filled with this oscillation between believing in the love she felt and fearing it.

"But what was it that led us to Jesus? Was it not a feeling?" She asked this in a podcast interview we did, and she's spot on here.

Was it not a feeling that led me to follow Jesus? A sense in my body, an electricity of endless love and compassion, that had me caught up in the joy of the Spirit? I can remember the moment clear as day.

It is heartbreaking that faith leaders will use our emotions as leverage to trap us in their cults of personality and then shame us for experiencing emotions after that. "If you feel your heart pounding, that's the Holy Spirit!" Or, maybe it's my body responding to stimuli and the pressure to perform my spiritual experience in a way that looks socially acceptable to the crowd I'm sitting in.

The verse that my brain and my upbringing scream is, "The heart is deceitful above all things." And then my heart whispers, "Before I formed you in your mother's womb, I knew you." Which is it, pastor? The Bible is full of delightful contradictions like this, and none of y'all seem to be able to square that.

...

I had the best sex of my life at a festival.
(What a way to start a story, right?)

Never in a thousand billion years did I think it'd be possible for me to have such an impromptu hook up outside of some sort of dating app. The world is full of wonder.

We met on the first evening of a festival. He called me over to a table with his friends to ask an irrelevant and arbitrary question, which he later revealed to be a ploy to talk to me. Honestly, when I saw him and heard his voice, I couldn't tell you if he was queer or not. Is he flirting with me or is he nice? This is question I ask with most kind men I speak to.

I resolved that he was just being nice and returned to my friends. But I kept running into him on the festival grounds, started learning more about what he did and realized that he was a freaking saint, doing the Lord's work of helping queer youth in rural Alabama. Indeed, a heart of gold. He ended up coming to all of my talks, ranging from owning our faith to sex positivity. There was a little bit of flirtation, but I was not about to let myself entertain the idea that anything could happen for me because I simply "didn't do those things."

And frankly I thought he was completely out of my league.

The final evening of the festival, while Amy Grant was singing her hits to an enraptured crowd of post-evangelicals, I saw him. Walking up to him with a few drinks in my system and a micro-dose of shrooms, I said, "Hey stranger." Which feels like a sexy thing, I think? He smiles his perfect smile, cutting through his perfectly trimmed, gingery beard. We shared some kind of small talk, and then we embraced.

Now, let me paint a picture for you:

He's a granola dude. I'm talking Chacos, Patagonia hiking shorts, and athletic wear polo shirt that shows off his perfectly sculpted chest. And he looks stunning in this. Me? I'm rocking the queer Christian Coachella outfit: short shorts, low cut shirt, floral kimono that I borrowed from my girlfriend, Sarah, a gold fanny pack, and a big floppy hat.

In my mind, boys like him are not interested in girls like me. So, it's not even on my radar that he could be interested. But, as fate would have it, as I was walking around, my fanny pack had settled over my crotch, and when we embraced, there was some extra pressure on our groins. And in my very brave (possibly stupid and quite inebriated) state, I said to him, "Just so you know, that's my fanny pack your feeling, not my penis."

I shit you not, he responded with, "Well, I wouldn't mind if it was."

In a snap, I sober up and without thinking, I ask, "Do you want to come back to my tent with me?"

"Yes," he says with a very matter of fact smile.

We go back to the tent, start fooling around, and as clothes start to come off, he tells me that he doesn't have sex with people he doesn't know. And I say, "Well, do you want to get to know me?" I scooch over, making room for him on this tiny cot in this oversized tent. We talk for the next hour. I think about everything. Family, what we want out of life, where we see ourselves in five years, what our last relationships were like, our mutual desire for ethical non-monogamy. I swear, it's like I found the most perfect human, and we were here together. At this point, even if we don't have sex, I'm just thankful I got to bond with someone in this way.

Just as the conversation begins to lull, he moves down towards my jeans and starts undoing my belt. Yaddah yaddah. For what also feels like a good hour or so, we made love. I don't say that about every sexual encounter, but for this one y'all...

We.
Made.
Love!

And it felt like magic.

The whole thing. Meeting just days prior, having all this natural chemistry, being able to talk about the deep waters of our hearts, and then being able to give ourselves this gift of deep intimacy. The way he held my body, both strong and soft, allowed me to let go in a way that I've never felt since. "It was a feeling of freedom, of seeing the light. It's Ben Franklin with the key and the kite."[17]

After we both finished, we lay there in the sweaty afterglow. In the distance, I could faintly hear the people at the beer and hymns tent, joyfully and loudly singing, "How great Thou art! How great Thou art..." in glorious four-part harmony.

Deeply looking at each other, lying on his chest, and then him on mine, we kept talking for another half an hour before we asked what time it was. Our friends were probably looking for us. (Not true. Our friends were wasted somewhere in the campground.)

We got up, got dressed, and kept kissing because it just felt so good. We promised to stay in touch, and then we exited the tent. He went and took a dip in the nearby stream. I went to the dance party to see my friends and brag a little bit.

I just had the best sex of my life.

For the first time, I was naked and unashamed.

...

Why am I telling you these stories? Why am I leaning more heavily into experience and not into reinterpreting scripture to make it fit our modern sensibilities?

---

[17] It's a quote from Hamilton. If you haven't seen it or heard it by now, what's wrong, sis? Who hurt you?

Because for us to move into a faith that is dynamic and informed by our actual lived experiences, we must actually include our lived experiences, seeing them as a holy text. We must see our lives as authoritative, not as a way to dictate a new morality or to fundamentalize our experiences as a new kind of mythical norm, but to see our experiences as essential data worthy paying attention to.

What if I could have believed the data my body was giving me when I kissed G for the first time? That feeling of goodness and electricity and coming alive. What if I was able to let that be a marker of what God had made? How much time would it have saved me? How much of my shame could I have undone in the moment, rather than agonizing for years?

We've been told and conditioned to not trust our bodies or our desires. We've been told that we are sin to our core, but I cannot believe that. If I am sin to my core, then I am doomed. I will always want destructive things. I will not want for my own good or the good of others.

My experience tells me a different story. My Gospel story that God is telling with my life tells a different story, and it is this:

The more I learned to trust my own body, to listen to Her desire, to give voice to His desire, to hold Them in their fear, the more I hear the voice of God, the more I understand the Universe's desire for this world, the more I am comforted by Love.[18]

I have learned that happiness is a marker of the Spirit, and we need to stop labeling it as evil. I've learned that asking for what I want is not selfish.

I believe that we are Love to our core. Do we have the propensity to mess things up, to commit errors, to sin against one another, ourselves, and the earth? Yes. But because we are Love to our core, we can change. We can repent. We can change our minds.

Repent, beloved. Change your minds about your body and your feelings. Set yourself free from the expectations placed on you by a religion that was founded and controlled by those mythical norms.

---

[18] My friend Jamie Lee Finch introduced me to the idea that my body is my partner, not just some random assortment of cells or a mere vessel for my mind. So, I refer to my body with all the pronouns I like, including She, Him, and Them. And I capitalize the pronouns because my body is holy and contains the Holy. That's why I talk about my body this way.

Your body is good.
Your desire is good.

I told you all of these stories to say that I think sex can be a sacrament: a way that we experience the things of the Spirit through a physical manifestation. For me, engaging in sex has allowed me to face my own shame about my body and my desire. Having sex allowed me to see how I was selfish, and also how I've used sex as a way to unknowingly manipulate others in relationship. Having sex has given me opportunities to experience real vulnerability and give grace to people who need it.

Since I've changed my mind about sex, repented of my shame and internalized queerphobia, I find the fruit of the Spirit. I've become a better friend and partner.

Honestly, having sex made me a better Christian.

8
HOLY. TRUE. RELATIONSHIP.

I stopped lying after a breakup. About everything. About who I wanted to be, where I wanted to go, what I wanted to do. Everything. In this particular relationship, I had hurt him, and he had hurt me. We were caught in a codependent cycle of trauma bumping into trauma, reopening scars, and operating from wounds so deep in the other that we often couldn't tell where one of us began and the other ended. For some folks, that last sentence sounds like a dream or a fairy tale.

Believe me when I tell you, to lose yourself in another person is to build for yourself a prison of premeditated resentments.

What I understood about relationships I had learned from my family of origin. You are to fight as long and as hard as you can to make it work because God hates divorce, not to mention the dread of having to tell everyone you know that your relationship failed. (And then imagine trying to figure out how to or if to talk about it on the internet.) That being said, in hindsight, I can see how scared I was both to stay with him and also to leave him.

I told him I loved him, and in my mind, love meant I had to stay. He was vulnerable. I could protect him. I could save him. I could fix him. If I could be patient enough, we'd make it to the other side of the hard season. But the thing is that our entire relationship was a hard season. We spent more time working on our relationship than actually being in one. Being that this was my first very serious relationship and that we decided to put our shit on Instagram, there was an added pressure to be the perfect queer Christian couple. Our relationship didn't belong to just him and me, but always the audience. It became another performance to keep up.

In my mind, a breakup meant all the people who told me that gay relationships don't work because "they go against God" would be right. I would be fuel for their fire, and that could not be allowed.

But who said that a relationship which ends is a relationship that has failed? My parents? My old church? My former pastors, who don't even know that I'm cohabiting before marriage with another practicing homosexual? Cosmo Magazine? Culture at large?

And didn't we *just* get done talking about how all the rules put on to us by the Church and society aren't actually real?

Do you see where we are going with this?

Just like our thoughts around different kinds of theology, I think we have to deconstruct and reconstruct how we do relationships. The monogamy prescribed by romance novels, romcoms, and Christian purity culture point us codependent, shallow, controlling relationships that we sometimes jokingly refer to as the ole ball and chain. Still, I believe there's some sort of saying about how all jokes have truth in them.

In reality, marriage has become the idol of the Church. It is the way the Church has managed our sexual desire and our desire for connection. Thus, it's become a way the Church has exerted control over many by way of prescribing a mythical norm of what marriage should be.

Think about it: so many of our churches create an entire model of their church based on the idea that marriage and the nuclear family is the default. They buy into the mythical norm. You've got the young adult small groups, which are really just holy mixers for horny twenty-somethings who are ready to bone. Then you've got the young married couples' group, the young families group, the empty nesters and then apparently you just become a part of the old folks group at some point.

But what of single folks? Be it due to their conviction to remain celibate or just a person who is single for one reason or another, where do they fall? Why are old folks relegated to some other ministry when their wisdom can be gleaned from? Also, why aren't we letting kids and babies be a part of our beloved communities? You'd never know it was a problem because the folks who do fall through the cracks generally drift away from churches. They couldn't fit into the false narrative that has been spun for us.

Even on the other side of coming out and deconstructing and, yes, even after complaining about this, I still possess this intense desire to be married. It's hard for me to tell if it is because of a legitimate desire to connect with someone on a deeply emotional, physical, sexual, spiritual level, or if it is because I grew up in a culture that taught me that holiness looked like two people, two rings, a kiss, and some cake before my love for another person could be legitimate in the eyes of God.

Maybe it's a little of both.

...

People who argue with me are really concerned about Genesis, about the man and woman becoming "one flesh." They get real testy with me when I tell them that this verse is not actually talking about perceived correctness in anatomical fittedness for sexual intercourse. (Read: it has nothing to do with a penis penetrating a vagina). Instead, it has to do with kinship.

Dr. James V. Brownson, in his book *Bible Gender Sexuality,* unpacks the misconceptions about what it means to be "one flesh." There is more connotation of sex, according to Brownson, in the word Hebrew word _dabaq_, which is what is translated into English as *cling.* This word is used over 54 times in the rest of the Old Testament, and nowhere else does it have a sexual connotation to it. Only here in Genesis did theologians arbitrarily assign a sexual meaning to the word *cling,* based on *our* own cultural understanding of *our* language, rather than the original usage.

This is not to say that to have "one flesh," that this unique and deep kinship does not include a sexual relationship, because it can, especially in the case of Genesis. I mean, if I saw bone of my bone walking around the garden, it is likely that I too, as an allosexual person, would wanna bone. But in other places in scripture where similar language is used, this kinship is not sexual.

Ruth "clings" to Naomi and asks her not to send her away.

Jacob calls Laban "bone of my bone" before setting up the dividing line between their two lands.

Neither of these relationships are erotic in nature. (As much as I want Ruth and Naomi to be a lesbian unrequited love story, the proof doesn't exist.)

Holy. True. Relationship.

However, in both of these passages, kinship means more than passive cordiality towards another. It means more than merely wanting to be near someone. It is "the desire to overcome aloneness, the longing for intimacy, to know and be known, to live one's life with others... Genesis 2:24 speaks of profound longings that are not merely sexual in character. They are at the bottom of longings for human community and fellowship, and these longings may express themselves in a variety of forms elsewhere in Scripture, in a variety of gendered relationships."[19]

The desire to be known, to be connected, and even the desire to have sex is a normal part of the human experience. It is part of the beauty of our creation. But because we've been given a twisted perspective of how relationships work, one that is rooted in domination or ownership of one another rather than mutuality and actual trust, we've ended up repeating cycles of behavior which have led us to where we are today.

I learned that I should seek to lose myself in another person because this life was never about me anyway. It was only ever about the Kingdom. And by the Kingdom, my leaders unknowingly meant their kingdoms and not God's. I think, subconsciously, I attempted to lose myself in another person so they could distract me from the fact that I didn't like the person I was, that *I* did not love the person I was. How could I? I was a terrible no good sinner. It'd be lucky if I could find a woman to marry this mess of a man I was. And when I met her, I would devote my all to her. Because that is what I knew I had to do.

This, my dear friends, is the environment that breeds codependent relationships. Based around false peace, following rules, making everyone happy except for you. So many of us who left that space wonder why we struggle to create healthy attachments to others, and we really shouldn't. We learned it from the Church.

No matter what you felt, your devotion to the local church really was all that mattered. As long as you showed up, and of course count it all joy as you go thru, but never ever actually ask why. Jump into these relationships in this particular way only, and don't deviate from it because it's sin.

In my midtwenties, as I was beginning to take my fifth year of undergrad, my timeline was filled with people getting engaged. So many diamonds. So many couples who you were rooting for. In fact, at the time

[19] James V. Brownson, *Bible. Gender. Sexuality.* Pg. 88.

I'm writing this, I've been to 74 weddings over the course of my life. (Yes, I've counted.) Now, as I enter my thirties, so many of my friends are getting divorced. Something we never could have saw coming and something we swore would never happen to us cause, duh, we're good Christians. For most of them, it's a good move, and most of them are shaking off any weird shame about it because there's nothing to be ashamed of. But I remember feeling so bad about not being married in my early twenties. It was like there was something deficient in me. So when I got with my first boyfriend, you bet I hung on as tight as I could.

I think I stayed with my first partner as long as I did because I was operating from that script that told me that if I wasn't married by a certain age, I was fucked. But that script was written for straight, white, cisgender people with money. I am not those things. Why did I try to fit a part in a script that wasn't written for me?

Because nothing else had been written. I didn't know anything else was possible. It took me seeing someone else living life a different way to understand that another approach was not only possible but necessary.

...

Living in Atlanta affords you some pretty great queer community if you know where to look. One unusually warm evening, I ended up in a community discussion group in a hot, cinderblock building on the west side. There was no AC in the space, but we didn't mind. We were there for the depth of conversation and the cupcakes.

The topic was on how our cultural obsession with romance had contributed to a culture that put deep, intimate friendships on the back burner. Once you put those friendships on the back burner, you had permission to turn that burner off. Because why do you need those other friendships when you have this one person who can be your absolute everything? You don't, right? Because that's what marriage is for. To complete you. Yet we all know that's not how it works. We want that to be true so badly. Were it only that simple.

The workshop leader posed a question to us that blew open my mind, and to this day, shapes how I form relationships. "What would happen if we treated our lovers more like our friends and our friends more like our lovers?"

I'm not saying that you and all your friends should bang each other (unless you want to, in which case, use a good lube). What I am saying is that this idea could bring equity back to our relationships, and it could begin to tear down the idol that we've made of monogamous marriage.

We have to begin by looking at the mythical norm of relationships and the assumptions we have about them. Within a romantic partnership, there is an assumption that your relationship must look a certain way. Mainly, your partner typically has a monopoly over your time, your energy, your money, your attention, your body, and so on. This is your person. You are theirs and they are yours. You plan your lives around them, you drop everything for them, you enmesh yourself with them, and you become an unhealthy version of "one flesh."

Furthermore, there is an assumption that your partner is entitled to your body, to sex, not to mention your loyalty in every area, not just in the bedroom. At least, that is how many relationships operate.

Now, look at your friendships, like the really, really deep ones. There's this idea that you tell your closest friends everything. You tell them the brutally honest truth because they can handle it. They are people you can fight with and not be afraid they are going to walk out or seek retribution. At the end of the day, you've got a love that's deeper than this surface bullshit going on. They are the people who are with you through thick and thin.

But if your significant other calls, wants to hang out or simply wants something from you, their needs take precedence over your friends because, again, that's your person.

Let's apply the question. What would happen if we treated our friends more like our lovers?

What if we dedicated time to our friends? What if we did beautiful things for them, listened deeply, and had healthy physical touch between us? What if we were willing to help them financially when they were in a rough spot? What if we celebrated anniversaries and took trips and were dedicated to loving our friends as hard and as much as we did our lovers?

What would happen if we treated our lovers more like our friends?

What if we told the truth to our partners? What if we were willing to be brutally honest about the things we've done and the things we wanted?

What if we weren't afraid that our partners were going to leave us when we got into a fight?

This is not a pass to shirk on responsibility or to go hang out with your friends because you haven't dealt with the issues with your partners. This is a call to reorient ourselves to all of our relationships. It's a call to love each other more by not making idols of our partners and not making our friendships mere pawns in our insecure game of life-chess.

...

Even after coming out, there was still this narrative in my head that happy looked like getting hitched. I was incomplete, or at least my happiness was incomplete, without a spouse and possibly a kid. That narrative was the mythical norm, telling me that sure it was fine that I was gay now. However, I was still nothing because who the hell would want to love a twenty-four-year old sexually inexperienced man with gender questions and a trauma-induced gag reflex?

Even if we don't say it out loud, even if we say loud and proud that we feel satisfied on our own, that we understand that marriage won't complete us, we still are longing to have someone stand across from us with a poster board reading in all block text, "YOU COMPLETE ME."

The bad theology at work here is that marriage is the norm, and our whole purpose here is to continue coupling off, rather than coming closer in to beloved community.

Contrary to what the Southern Baptist Convention, Jerry Falwell Jr., or The Handmaid's Tale would tell you; the point of marriage is not procreation. Nor is it to create a more complete picture of God through the bonds of holy matrimony. Even by conservative theological standards, to argue that marriage is necessary to more fully experience God would be to say that Jesus was incomplete in himself. If He lacked in his humanity, then He would not know what it was to be human. Thus, He would be disqualified as the perfect lamb to be slain because His divine nature would have given him an unfair advantage.

This is where we could get into a whole question of whether or not Jesus was God or human or both or neither, but that's a different book. Let's hone in on the fact that Jesus, understood to be single for His entire earthly life (though this is also unverifiable and contested by certain gnostic gospels), demonstrates to us what it is to be a new kind of humanity, fully united and in communion with God, fully integrated and motivated by Love. Even if Jesus had a spouse, I wonder why that would diminish His divinity in the minds of some. Why is it that generating more love in the world could have made Him less divine?

This isn't me knocking marriage at all. Marriage is dope. I'm merely curious as to how holy matrimony became more important than holy living, more important than knowing who God created you to be.

The reason it may sound like I'm going after marriage's jugular is because of what we were made to believe about it. I don't want to destroy marriage. I just want to take it off the pedestal. I want to smash the idol that marriage has become.

We learned there was only one correct way of relating to one another person in romantic love was to be lost in them. In this other person, we invest our own power over our happiness and joy. In them, our spouse, we long to move and breathe and have our being. We are looking for them to be the rescuer. We are told that our partner is supposed to be all the things we are not in order to make up for our own inadequacies.

But the example of Jesus' humanity and our status as co-heirs with Christ would lead me to believe that we are not incomplete. Instead, we have the potential to be boundless, endless flowing rivers of Living Water if we could just remember that we always were.

We invest so much faith in our romantic partners and lovers. We expect so much of them. We are wrapped up in fantasies of who we think they are and who we think they could be instead of seeing them as they actually are. We don't see them as the very human person who, very much like us, is trying to figure out what they want. We hold them to a higher standard than everyone else, which in reality is a fearful projection covering up the truth we don't want to admit.

We don't even live up to our own standards of what we believe romantic partnership should be, and thus we react to it when we see it in our partner. We have less grace for them because we don't have enough grace for ourselves.

The kind of relationship where we regard someone from a higher position than us is what *A Course in Miracles* calls a *special relationship*. Special relationships are not special because of how you treat someone. They are special because the kind of love you give them comes with attachments.

There is a promise or exchange attached to it. We do it with all sorts of relationships. "When you give your power to someone whom you *assume* is closer to beauty, talent, power, success, wealth, wisdom, or God than you are, you have a special relationship..."[20]

We do it with our spouses, our parents, our lovers, celebrities, sports teams, megachurches, denominations, brands, as well as any other religion and spirituality. We give over our authority to them. We make them responsible for our happiness and well-being and self-esteem and worth. When the person on the receiving end of this special kind of love, we resent them because they did not live up to what we thought they were, or instead, they were not who we projected them to be. We feel betrayed.

Now there is so much to be said about misrepresenting yourself, like when a church does that bullshit bait-and-switch, "We love gay people but disagree with their lifestyle." That is called lying. (It could also be called theological catfishing, if you're feeling spicy.)

But how many of us still hold on even after we've heard the lie? After we have been shown who they are? After the red flags go up? After the cards are on the table and the truth has been spoken? We think we are powerful enough that we can change the church, the person, the lover, the spouse, the work culture, whatever it is that we've elevated in our minds. We think that if we just give enough of ourselves to this other person, they will be overwhelmed by love and poof! Magic. They are better. And we did it. We fixed them because we are *such* good people.

Beloved, it was never your job to fix them. It was never your job to convince them of your worth. You should first convince yourself of your worth before anyone else. That is how you heal. That's how we heal this whole thing.

In the same way that we have to divest our power from structures and systems that have power over us, we must do this with our relationships. We must allow those whom we've made idols of to come down from the pedestal and restore them to the beauty of their divine humanity. We must bring them back down to our level and see them as just as beloved as we are, not more beloved.

---

[20] Alan Coen, *A Course In Miracles Made Easy*, pg 60.

The opposite of special relationships is not non-special relationships where no one has labels, plunging us into a free love sexual paradise (unless that's something you're into!). No, the answer to *special relationships,* according to *A Course in Miracles,* is *holy relationships.* Admittedly, this sounds a lot like that old adage we had in ex-gay therapy world wherein they often said that the opposite of homosexuality wasn't heterosexuality. Holiness was. So, if you're triggered, take a deep breath. We're not going in that direction.

The holy relationship is one in which you do not see yourself as without or in need of completion. You, in and of yourself, in your beautiful created incarnation, are a reflection of God's fullness. Your body is a vessel for the Holy Spirit. In holy relationship, you do not look to other people to fulfill you as you might in a codependent or special relationship. You find your peace and joy and solace and happiness, not in a relationship or another person's delight in us, but rather the delight you find in your own incarnation. The love you have for yourself is so much that it is multiplied between you and all of creation, especially in those whom you love. We see these things in the truth that we are already loved, whole, and created with a purpose. Nothing can shake that.

The purpose of any partnership, be it romantic or platonic or otherwise, "is to not offset each other's deficient, but to honor and express your already-existing sufficiency."[21] It is a mutual outpouring of energy from the overflow of one's infinite connection to Love which serves as the flow between our relationship.

Is it always as clean and neat as that? Of course not. We are not perfect, and we are not expected to be. We are, however, expected to try. We will hurt one another because we all have been hurt. Just because we understand the principle of holy relationships does not mean we will turn around and fix our relationships with a snap of a finger. The work of building holy relationships, equitable relationships based in mutuality, respect, and joy starts by getting really fucking honest.

...

During that breakup I was talking about at the front end of this chapter, my best friend suggested that I write down a list of things that gave me hope about my relationship. He then suggested I write down the things that would need to change if we were to stay together. The things that gave

---

[21] Coen, pg 61

me hope were beautiful. It reminded me of the reasons I fell in love with him, the reasons I fought for this relationship as long as I had.

The second list, the one with things that would have to change, to say the least, was longer than my first.

I got honest. Not even brutally honest, just regular honest. I named how I felt hurt. I named the habits he had, which were causing us to have a rift between us. I owned how my own fuck-ups had impacted how he was acting towards me. We discussed we were codependent. I said that as long as we stayed together, I didn't think he could heal because he didn't know how to forgive me. Furthermore, I had to admit that *I* couldn't heal with him.

I loved him so much, and at the same time I had to go. I knew it was the right thing to do. My biggest regret in all of it was that I didn't have this conversation sooner. Were I able to name my needs, desires, wants, and boundaries sooner, I may have, at a minimum, saved both of us a lot of time and perhaps some heartbreak.

With no plan of where I'd live or how I'd pay for my own place or literally anything else, I left. I had a few friends ask politely if I had a plan for where I'd go next, and I didn't. My friend's couch was my first crash landing site, but beyond that was just trusting that maybe God had not forgotten me. Guilt still racked my body, though. The script I had lived by for so long, on how good Christian relationships looked, told me I had failed.

I didn't keep my partnership together, and therefore my worth was lessened. Shame kept me smoked up in bed for weeks, binging on video games and boxed wine. I had gotten myself here. It was my fault.

Maybe some of it was. But then again, did it matter? In the grand scheme of things, perhaps not, but at that moment, the pain was so great. It takes a lot for someone who struggles with chronic depression to remember that it won't always feel like the worst thing. And what would blaming myself do for anyone? It would not lessen my pain any more than it would have reduced my ex's pain.

For a whole year and some change afterward, my therapist pointed out how I continually brought him up. I would bring up how I hurt him. I would talk about how he was so emotionally manipulative. I would talk about my inability to tell the truth about what I wanted. It was a constant circle of violence against myself and him and me again and him again. Even after we broke up, our special relationship, my special love entwined with special hate for the ways he made me feel vulnerable was holding on strong in the recesses of my mind. Then my therapist said something that pissed me off and set me free all at once.

"You know, your obsession over the ways you hurt your ex is just your way of punishing yourself again and again, so you don't have to do the hard work of forgiving yourself."

Isn't that always the way? It was true. My ex was gone. He couldn't inflict any more pain on me and I couldn't inflict any more pain on him. The pain I felt he may have handed to me, but I was the one who chose to hang on for it. But I felt like I deserved it. I deserved, on some level, to remember what a fucking dirtbag I was. I clung to it as hard as I clung to the self-hate I learned from the church.

That is how I felt. That's how so many of us think. But what is the truth? What does God say about us? I hear the voice of Jesus asking us, "What is easier, to say 'your sins are forgiven,' or 'pick up your mat and walk?'"

Answer: the first one. It really is as simple as that.

Sitting in my therapist's office, in something I can only describe as a move of the Holy Ghost, I suddenly had a vision. In my minds eye, I saw myself sitting across from a version of me from a few years ago. This envisioned version of myself looked tired; looked worn. I looked me dead in the eyes. I looked at myself, and said, "You are forgiven. You are forgiven. You are forgiven." As I pronounced forgiveness over myself, I felt the tense place at the base of my stomach finally release. The pain of all I had carried welled up in my eyes and wailed from my lungs.

It was the ugliest of ugly cries, but my God did it feel incredible to let that shit go. What is so beautiful is that at the same moment, I could feel the tension of holding on to that pain release. I could forgive him because I had forgiven myself for the ways I messed up. I forgave myself for placing himself above me, expecting more of him than he could give. I forgave myself for making my relationship the center of my life instead of my connection to Love. I had finally taken him down from the pedestal. He was like me.

He was beloved.

And I was beloved.

And we were both free.

My only regret is that I never got to tell him how sorry I was. For how I placed him above myself. For how I chose to see him as anything other than who he was. For how I lied to him. For how I betrayed him. For how I wish we could still be friends now.

And that's okay. Sometimes you don't get to say sorry to the person. Sometimes the bridges aren't rebuilt after they are burnt. But forgiveness is never about restoration or reconciliation. That's ideal, sure, but the point of forgiveness is your own personal freedom. You can cut the ties to the past that have kept you bound.

This can be with a person, to a church, a pastor, a mother or father, or any other person who hurt you. But it starts with you looking at yourself and realizing you did the best you could. Given your life, your story, what you've carried, you've only ever been able to do your best. Even if you weren't doing your best, even if the way you operated at the time was totally fucked up, it doesn't matter. What is important is that you're here. You're reading these words. And now you know what is possible.

What would it be like to forgive yourself? What would it be like to look at the person or the religion or the church who has hurt you, and say, "What you did wasn't right. And.... I am tired. Tired of fighting something that isn't even engaged with my life. Tired of fighting for something I felt was owed me. Tired of being angry with something that I cannot change. Today, I rest. Today, I release. Today, I forgive myself for thinking I could find myself in you. Today, I forgive myself for the ways I saw you as anything but who you were and what you are. I forgive you, and I release you to the Holy Spirit."

This can be the beginning of healing. This can be the place you work from instead of for.

Do we still need to do work? Still need to rally and protest and reform? Yes, of course. Until Kin'dom come. But rather than working from a deficit of love and energy, heal yourself. Create for yourself a new foundation of love and belonging, one that isn't contingent upon a group or a church or another person or success or a movement even. Your ground is God. Your beginning is belonging to Love. Your power is infinite connection.

If we can learn to work from Love, in everything, and not for Love, we will be able to make the changes we so desperately wish for.

Holy. True. Relationship.

INTERLUDE III
A SHORT STORY
"THE WHITE DENIM JACKET"

There were once a particular people who lived at a very particular time who all wore a very particular kind of white denim jacket.

Some people bedazzled their jacket with rhinestones, others with patches. It didn't matter how you wore it, as long as you wore it. It was a cultural marker. People just wore the same jacket. Same cut, same style, same color. It was what united these people. Everyone wore the jacket. And everyone loved the jacket.

Every child born to these people grew up knowing that one day, they too would get their very own white denim jacket. They looked forward to getting their own, knowing that it meant that they also were accepted and beloved, a part of their people. Some of them even wore smaller versions of the jacket until they grew into the standard jacket that everyone wore.

After a time, one of the children finally grew into a Young Person, old enough to put on the white denim jacket. It was already marked with fine stitching and jewels. It was beautiful, and they were incredibly proud to wear their jacket, and they often would show it off to people they would meet.

"You look sensational!" the people would exclaim. "You should be so proud of how pristine your white denim jacket is. You are exactly like us and we love you."

The Young Person loved them too. They felt safe and loved. They knew their place among their people.

Each week, the Young Person would go to the public square and gather with their people. They would share stories, good things and hard things, sad things and joyful things. No matter what happened, the Young Person knew that they belonged. The white jacket remined them that everyone belonged.

One evening, the Young Person saw in the distance what looked like a light flickering in the distance. The light looked like it was dancing. They'd never seen anything like it. It felt faint, but it was almost as if they heard music. It was as if the light called to them.

When the Young Person asked their people about the light in the distance, the people told him to not pay it any attention.

"Don't bother looking there. Outside of our boundaries of our city is a wild world. It is scary and lonely, desolate, full of weeping and gnashing of teeth. But fear not! We have what you need here, and we will protect you no matter what."

The Young Person heard what their people said and believed them.

To be safe and loved and to listen was all the Young Person ever knew. And for a time, they listened.

And yet, the Young Person was curious. What could be so dangerous? Surely, it was not that scary!

The Young Person could not get the light out of their head, nor the faint sound of music. They had to go find out what it was. So, in the night, the Young Person went beyond the boundaries of where their people lived to see what was in the wild.

As the Young Person journeyed ever closer to where the light seemed to sit, the music became louder, as did who was making it. They came upon a group of wild people, dancing around a fire. The wild people all looked different.

The wild people were fat and skinny. They were dark and pale. They were everything in-between too!

The wild people were eating and drinking with one another. This was extravagance the Young Person had never seen before, and they were amazed.

The Young Person asked, "Who are you? And how did you all come to look like this? And why are you dancing so wildly?"

The wild people answered, "We're the Wild People! Some of us looked like you before we tasted it."

"Tasted what?" The Young Person asked.

"The bread that Grandmother makes, of course!" the Wild People responded. "Come! Are you hungry? You can have some if you want."

The Wild People sat the Young Person down at the table and passed him some bread. The Young Person was hungry, and so they took and ate some of the bread. It tasted sweet, like honey.

It was so delicious, and the Young Person lamented that they didn't have anything like this where they came from.

"Well, you are always welcome to eat with us," the Wild People said to the Young Person.

And so, they ate and they drank and they danced, and when the sun was coming up, the Young Person said goodbye to the Wild People and returned home.

Upon returning home, people asked the Young Person, "Why is your jacket so dirty? Where have you been that you've stained it?"

"I met the Wild People!" the Young Person. "And we danced and ate and drank, and I felt so good!" The Young Person began to dance like they did around the fire, remembering how good it felt to feel good.

But the people didn't understand.

"Your jacket is so dirty! You need to clean it before you come out in public again; otherwise, people will stare. No one will want to be around you if you look and act like this."

The Young Person understood and rushed home, embarrassed. They washed their white denim jacket, trying to remove the marks left from the celebration of the Wild People. But, no matter how they worked, there were still a few marks left.

The Young Person scowled, sighed, and put on the white denim jacket, and returned to their people.

But night after night, the Young Person would remember the Wild People. They remembered the bread and the drink. They remembered how much fun it was to be out there, moving their body, and how good it felt to feel good.

"I know I mustn't," the Young Person reasoned with themselves, "But I want to. And it made me feel so good… I know, I'll just clean my jacket before I come back home. My people will never suspect that I have left and come back.

So, as the people of the city retired, the Young Person left their home, heading back outside the boundaries of where their people lived to meet with the Wild People again.

"We are so happy to see you!" the Wild People exclaimed. "What took you so long to come? You know you're always welcome to eat with us."

The Young Person smiled, taking the bread and eating, its sweet taste returning.

For a few nights the Young Person went back and forth to the Wild People's camp, each time, remembering to not stay too long. They snuck back into the city, back to their home, and cleaned their white denim jacket furiously so know one would suspect him of disobeying the rules.

However, one evening, the Young Person was having such a wonderful time, they didn't realize that time had slipped away, and the sun was coming up. Without a word, the Young Person bolted across the wilderness, back to his city.

When the Young Person returned to the city, people were already awake and saw him. They were distraught at the sight of the Young Person, shamefully returning back from the forbidden world outside.

"How could you do this again? Why do you disrespect us like this? After the care we have given you! After all, we have taught you about living in the community, this is how you repay us?"

"I'm sorry!" the Young Person exclaimed. "I didn't mean to offend. I just wanted to dance and move and feel good." The people looked at them with disdain and disgust.

"Clean your jacket," the people commanded. "Or do not be seen."

The Young Person, fearful, returned to their dwelling, took off their jacket and began to clean it with bleach, removing any trace of the Wild People from the jacket.

When the Young Person woke up the following morning, they pulled on their white denim jacket and noticed something strange. It didn't fit. It felt tight and uncomfortable.

They went to the people of the city and asked, "May I have a bigger size jacket? This one has become too small."

"No, everyone wears this jacket," the people said. He looked around at everyone wearing identical white denim jackets.

"Surely, there must be another? Something that will fit me better?"

"Everyone fits into the jacket," the people said. "Of course, it fits! Nobody needs a bigger one because this jacket is perfect. Everyone wears it."

The Young Person tugged on the sleeves, trying to get the jacket reach at least reach their wrists. The Young Person tried pulling it around their chest, but the buttons didn't even get close to the buttonholes.

"Please," the Young Person asked, "This is so tight, and I don't feel comfortable."

"But at least you are wearing the jacket," they responded, "and that's what is important."

The Young Person went home, feeling defeated.

Night after night, the Young Person looked out the window and saw the light of the fire, and they dancing, the sweat, the laughter, the fun they had, and how free the felt among the Wild People. But that wasn't where the Young Person belonged. They were not safe there, and they were only safe if they stayed where they were, listened to who was in charge, and behaved like every other good person who wore a white denim jacket.

The Young Person would often feel hungry but couldn't find it in themselves to eat. They smiled, did their daily work, showed up to the gatherings, and tried to do life normally among the people of the city so that there would be no strife or conflict among them, but inside they were sad.

The young person was filled with sorrow because they had tasted a sweet bread of honey, and they knew not when they'd eat it again. They were sad because they had danced and sang new songs, made new friends, and they didn't know when they'd sing anything new again.

One evening, as the day concluded, and the sun set, the Young Person thought about the bread, the dancing, the Wild People, and how it felt to be out there. The heartache was so great, the pull of the light too alluring, they left the boundaries of where their people lived to meet with the Wild People once again.

When the Young Person arrived, the Wild People asked, "Why is your face downcast, beloved?"

"My jacket no longer fits, and my people don't have a bigger size for me."

"Well, if it's uncomfortable, why not just take it off?"

"Everyone wears the jacket," the Young Person mindlessly repeated.

"But we do not wear the jacket," the Wild People responded.

The Young Person looked around. They had never noticed that the Wild People were wearing all sorts of jackets. Some with sleeves, some without. Some in bright colors, others in black. Some long, some short. Some were two jackets sewn together to make a whole new jacket.

Some folks didn't wear a jacket at all.

"You don't have to wear a jacket if it hurts to wear it," the Wild People said. And the Young Person gingerly removed the jacket, feeling the space to move their arms freely again.

"Something is different," the Wild People observed. "Have you grown?"

The Young Person examined their arms and legs. Their arms had grown strong from dancing in. the moonlight. Their legs had grown strong from the journey into the wilds, time and time again.

The Young Person had not noticed until they took off the jacket that it wasn't that jacket shrank.

The Young Person had grown.

And with their arms free, the Young Person danced with no jacket on. Their arms free in the moonlight, their skin sweating by the heat of the fire, their mouth wide in laughter.

Grandmother called everyone together, with her beautiful, patchwork jacket adorned with gold and beads and patches and symbols from all the jackets around the table.

She passed everyone some bread and poured everyone some wine.

And so, they ate and they drank and they danced, and when the sun was coming up, the Young Person said goodbye to the Wild People and returned to their home, smiling the entire way.

When he returned home, dirty denim jacket in hand, the people of the city saw them and immediately howled insults at them.

But the Young Person, feeling defiant, asked, "Why? Why does everyone wear the jacket? Why does it have to stay so clean? Why can't we wear what makes us feel good? Why do we have to stay within the boundaries of this city? I've been to the wilderness and there is not weeping but dancing!"

"Dancing is not allowed!" the people of the city said.

"Why not? Why can't I do what makes me feel good?

"Because," the people said, "You belong here, with us, and we love you. I know you think it's a burden, but that is the cost of being here. Everyone wears the jacket. Everyone stays. If you won't wear the jacket, you can't be seen."

"But my jacket doesn't fit anymore," the Young Person responded. "I've grown!"

"Of course, it does. The jacket fits everyone," the people of the city mindlessly repeated.

The Young Person, frustrated by the people, went back to their dwelling, throwing his once-beloved jacket on the ground, they wept because no one would listen to the pain he was in.

When night came, the Young Person grew hungry again. And so, without a second thought, they left the boundaries where their people lived to go meet with the Wild People once more.

When the Young Person arrived, the Wild People asked, "Where is your white denim jacket?"

"It no longer fit me," the Young Person said. "I was hoping maybe I'd make a new one here."

"Splendid!" The Wild People explained. "We'll show you all the materials we used!" The Young Person smiled as he surveyed the fire and the table and Grandmother, once again baking her bread.

"Are you hungry?" The Wild People asked. "You know you're always welcome to eat with us."

"I know," said the Young Person. "I know."

And so, they ate and they drank and they danced, and as the sun was coming up, the young person decided to stay for breakfast.

And then for lunch.

And then for dinner and dancing.

And the Young Person decided never to return to the city, to not go back to a place that forced them into any jacket that didn't fit. They chose to stay with the Wild People, becoming wild themself, and learning that to be wild meant to be free, and to be free meant to be happy.

The Young Person tried many different jackets on over the years but realized that dancing with their friends was more fun than fussing over what kind of jacket people wore. What was important was the dance.

The Young Person also learned how to bake Grandmother's bread, and they learned the taste of good wine, often serving it alongside Grandmother.

Sometime later, a stranger in a white denim jacket came to the fire.

"Hello!" The Young Person said, approaching the stranger.

"Are you hungry?" the Young Person asked the stranger, offering them some bread and wine and a seat at the table.

"You know, you're always welcome to eat with us."

The stranger smiled at the Young Person, taking a bite to eat of the bread and a drink of the wine.

"Oh!" the stranger exclaimed, hand to their mouth. "It taste like honey."

9
HONESTLY, THO

Did you ever see the movie *Saved?* It's about a young woman named Mary who finds out her boyfriend is gay. To save him from going to Hell for being gay, she ends up getting pregnant. This begins a series of events where Mary ends up in the company of the rejects of school, engaging in what the administration sees as bad behavior. The administration asks some of the pious and popular girls at school, girls who used to be friends with Mary, to see if they can talk some sense into her. The girls say they understand their task, but what happens in the following scene is both hilarious and also low-key triggering.

(Also, spoiler alert. But if you haven't seen *Saved* by now, you didn't want to see it.)

A car races up behind Mary as she is walking home from school and out pops the piety squad. The girls grab Mary, throw her in the van, and begin performing an exorcism. Mary exclaims that they are all fucking nuts and breaks free. The girls explain that they are only trying to help, to which Mary responds that they know nothing about love.

As she walks away, Mandy Moore's character, throws a Bible at Mary and says the iconic line, "*I am filled with Christ's love!* You're just jealous of my success in the Lord."

Mary picks up the Bible, and approaching Mandy says, "This... this is not a weapon, you idiot."

This scene is what so many of us fear will happen to us when we finally get honest about what we're all thinking and feeling. We're afraid that as we get more honest about how our life circumstance has caused us to question everything, people will start asking us questions. We're so scared we'll get pulled into the van and have people who claim to love us start casting out an evil spirit when really, it's just reasonable amounts of doubt within themselves they are afraid of confronting.

It's painful to have this happen, to realize that you're at odds with people you love. The first time I noticed this tension, I was living with some friends after my time as a missionary, serving my church, and working full time. But according to my pastor, I was also engaging in some low-key heresy.

My pastor, at the time, had told me that he didn't care what I believed, only that I understood why I believed what I did. And so, I got to work.

I'd begun considering that perhaps the Bible was not a monolith that could be interpreted and applied only one way. What's more, I started telling my friends that I believe that my heart was shifting. My mind was slipping away from what we always thought about being Christian meant, and if same-sex relationships could be God-honoring. It was a way for me to sort of dip my toes into the affirming waters without actually allowing myself to go total heretic.

It was all okay at first. My friends nodded along politely, not really taking a stance, saying that they didn't know if they agreed with me, but "what's important is Jesus." They always came back to that. Jesus was supposed to be the glue that held us together when our disagreements about things like doctrine didn't quite work out. Jesus was the essential belief we all had to keep, specifically that he was literally God, literally died and rose again. That act saved us from eternal damnation in Hell. At the time, I would've co-signed all of that. However, I was reading about racial justice and feminism at the time, and I was beginning to have misgivings about a lot of the things I was experiencing at church.

The more I spent time with him through the company of non-white, non-cis male thinkers and teachers, the more Jesus was revealing himself to be more and more inclusive, more and more radical. Being at my church began to feel like trying to pull on a jacket that was simply too small for how big my body of faith had grown. This was only impacted further by people God (I assume) kept bringing into our Church.

Gloria and Stef were a lesbian couple coming to our church at the time. Real talk, I avoided them like the plague because I knew how it worked. Proximity to active homosexual lifestyles equaled temptation to engage in the lifestyle myself. Even though I didn't actually think it was a sin for *them*, I knew for me, it was a no-go. My convictions were strong. I knew what I was meant for. I knew I was set aside for holiness.

Stef sent me a Facebook message one night after Saturday services, a night when I was leading worship. The message was short.

"God loves you as you are, and there's nothing to change."

Big gulp down my throat.

The desire for this to be true, to just accept that God loved me, and that was always enough, was so powerful that it hurt. It was a stream attempting to sweep me away when I was trying to hold on to the safety of my illusion. I knew I could let go, but what if I was wrong? I could not get over the fear that my desire was terrible. My body was bad. Anything I could dream up was probably not of God. I had to trust my leaders.

Yet seeing Gloria and Stef, even from a distance, was changing my mind. Their mere presence, being who they were, began to change me. When I saw them interacting with their son, I just saw love. I knew in my body that this was holy. There was no way that the love this family created could be anything but holy. That shook me.

How could these two be so free, I wondered. Why was it okay for them to be gay, but God had not given me that same peace? Why them and not me? It was part jealousy and part curiosity.

Around the same time, Virginia's state government voted to pass a law giving same-sex couples the right to get married in our state. I was genuinely happy about this, which also gave me pause. How could I be pleased about something my church (and myself, technically) said was a sin?

There was a fair bit of theological gymnastics I had to do to square it in my mind, but where I landed was an argument about authority and free will. If queer people didn't submit themselves to the authority of a church body, by extension, they did not submit themselves unto God. This being the case, the church has no room to speak into their lives or tell them what they should do, right? We are here to do good on the earth, to do good to people and for people, even those we disagree with because all people are God's children. Love matters more than agreeing. Respect matters more than being right.

This new position I had was due in no small part to Gloria and Stef. Seeing them, how they loved each other, how they loved their child, and how they loved me without barely knowing me changed my mind. I couldn't look at this issue without thinking of them. Why wouldn't I want them to have equal protection under the law? Why wouldn't I want them to get a fucking tax break for deciding to shack up and rear a child? Regardless of what people thought about issues of lifestyle and salvation, I don't think anyone could argue that improving the quality of someone's life was sinful.

Did I admit any of that to myself? Hell no. I had to keep it unemotional because emotions, according to my Evangelical upbringing, were proof that I couldn't think with a clear head and be objective. That's an argument used against folks (especially women) to gaslight us into thinking that our positions are unfounded simply because they are personal.

I kept it logical. I sidestepped deconstructing the bad theology in favor of something I merely saw as common sense. Folks who don't prescribe to your worldview aren't going to follow your precepts. So why don't we live and let live? Seemed moderate enough.

For me, what seemed moderate was a flaming liberal agenda that lit a warning fire in my pastor, enough to get me pulled into a meeting with him. I came to his office, quite unaware of what was happening or why I was there, and I could feel the energy of the room was tense. It was the feeling you have when you walk up to folks, and you know they were talking about you.

My pastor and I were close, and got lunch often, so part of me hoping it was just a check-in, as usual. But this time was different. The youth pastor, someone I counted as a friend and brother, was there to bear witness to this meeting. His face was grimaced, and he kept his eyes on the ground, and he remained silent the whole time.

"So, we read your article," the pastor began. The week before, I had published an article about why Christians should stay out of the marriage equality fight. It was pulled up on the computer monitor behind him. When I saw it, I knew it was about to get worse. The long and short of he had to say, basically, was I was wrong. I was approving of a sinful lifestyle, and therefore in sin myself. "God gave us marriage, and we cannot go against what God said marriage is."

I tried to argue that marriage is a cultural phenom that is present in almost every people group throughout the world, regardless of whether or not they had a "Biblical" definition of it. But he didn't and wouldn't hear me. He basically told me I was wrong, that to hold this position and belief was not just untenable, it was a willful sin. It was our duty as Christians to stand against the moral corruption of society, and I was hindering that stand.

Yet I hadn't done anything. I had shared an opinion. Was it not safe even to disagree on something non-essential to our salvation? We had always been challenged to explore why we believe, and I found that our time was better spent loving folks instead of making them feel like God didn't love them. Me thinking differently wasn't a big deal.

Except it was. It was a huge deal to my pastor that a popular parishioner within his congregation would make a public statement diminishing the role of the Church in the courts and in the cultural conversation. What if the teens I ministered to read it? What if other people saw it and it damaged their faith? (I argued that if a singular opinion could ruin someone's faith, then it was pretty weak faith, in my opinion, but that didn't seem to play too well with him.)

"For now, you're off the worship team." He was curt. I was stunned. It was the one place where I felt like I was home. It was the place I came alive. And he took it from me because I disagreed with him. I was being punished. Looking to my friend, the youth pastor, for any support and the only thing he offered was a sorrowful look. It was like looking into the eyes of one of my actual brothers after dad yelled at us. I wonder if he was scared. But regardless, he was either unwilling or unable to speak. I felt alone. I felt betrayed.

It was clear to me that Jesus was not the center of our world or our friendships or even our church. Towing the party lines was. It was our edict to appear as one in opinion, of one mind in thought and word, no matter what. There was no room for questions.

This was my van.

This was my exorcism.

This was having a bible thrown at me from someone who claimed to be filled with Christ's love.

My choices were clear. Either I could do what I was told and stop stirring the pot, or I could lose all of my rights, privileges, and opportunities as a member of my church. And for a while, I did. I stopped posting articles about stuff I was actually passionate about in favor of keeping the peace. Because it was more important, in the eyes of my pastor, to maintain the unity of the brotherhood no matter the cost. Even if some folks got hurt. And if they got hurt, it's because they simply couldn't handle the truth.

...

The more I look back on that time in my life, I don't think I experienced a deconstruction of my faith as much as I experienced a grand evolution of my faith. The roots all still look the same. Much of the language I have and use for my spiritual practice finds itself tracing paths back to Jesus. Or forward to Jesus, depending on how you look at it.

Sure, there was a sense that it kind of blew up. I mean, it did kinda feel like all the parts of my faith were on fire and burning my goddam flesh off, aka literal Hell. But not Hell, because it did not last forever. It was suffering. And it was a beautiful teacher.

I still hold on to Jesus. I can't really explain why beyond the pure feeling of "I don't want to let go." I don't want to give up Jesus because the Church has fucked up his image so bad, but sometimes it feels like there is this pressure to drop one or the other or both.

In queer spaces, I'm less likely to closely identify as a Christian because I know what that will trigger in other people. But when some asshole on twitter says that there's no such thing as a queer Christian, my immediate response is, "Fuck you and your white Jesus, I am a goddam Christian." Maybe part of it has to do with the sheer amount of time I've spent in the baptismal waters, so to speak. This is what I've known. Jesus has been my teacher since I was nine years old. I've been attempting to take on the mind of Christ my whole life, in one way or another. That's nothing to be embarrassed about. What a gift, honestly.

Seriously, having a religious language and two-thousand years of thought and argument to draw from? That's a lavish gift in many ways.

But at what point does a gift for one generation become the burden for the next? Like the industrial revolution. It was a gift that helped modernize the world. Now, it is a burden of our generation to figure out how to save our planet from our foreparents' "gift" of factories and production.

Western Europe saw its colonial and divine conquest as a gift to the world. A few hundred years later, we are still dealing with the aftermath of what our foreparents did to indigenous populations the world over. And frankly, we ain't "dealing" with it very well because power and church together make one dreadful and seemingly invulnerable beast.

The Christian faith has become that for me. I see and love all the good in it. I see how the story of Jesus, of the Christ, of a veil being torn in two to reveal that that separation from Love only existed in our minds. I see how other people have ruined it for others, used the name of my teacher, Jesus, to kill and to rape and to steal and to destroy those who lacked the power to defend themselves.

At what point does this thing become a barrier to what the Holy Spirit is actually trying to do? When will the yoke of keeping the Church alive be too heavy?

We are coming upon an age where we're learning to improvise like jazz musicians on the faith handed to us. The essence is there, but it is beginning to sound totally different than before, and it should. If we are transformed, our words will be, too. (And our music for that matter. We really need better worship music than this Jesus-is-my-boyfriend worship music CCM has been putting out for the better part of two decades.)

I believe we are getting to the end of our data collection. We're ready to be done with endlessly unpacking our spiritual and emotional baggage, and prepared to break camp and move forward. We are taking to heart the lesson of our brother Paul, who said that everything is permissible, but not everything is beneficial. We see that much of what we carried so far is not beneficial. We can pick out the authentic from the inauthentic, the truth from the lie, the valuable from the valueless. This is to our advantage. But while we can see truth, we are unable to internalize and be moved by it.

To us, it's data. It's a million considerations and what-ifs. It's feeling too traumatized to actually do the work of healing ourselves, let alone our communities. It is an epidemic of the most influential generation in history believing they are not at all able. We feel powerless.

And it does not have to be this way.

If we are to build a future and a faith that is going to sustain us in the decades to come, we must do the hardest thing.

We must begin.

We must begin to own our spiritual authority, begin making new spaces for beloved community to grow, begin telling the truth, begin letting our faith push us toward organizing ourselves around what will bring the most good for the most people.

We take what is given. We learn to improve it. We build it on purpose and with purpose in a way that we end the violence that has come against us. That's what we are trying to do with our economy, our transportation, and our justice movements, at least that is the progressive dream of many of our hearts. It is the heaven we strive to bring to the earth. Why not do this same thing with our faith? Why not improve our thoughts and get convicted about our actions? Why not work to make worship and faith environments so that they don't cause any more harm?

Beloved, it is because we are scared. We are scared that once we start pulling on the one thread labeled "doubt," the tapestry will fall apart. We are afraid that if we get honest about what is going on inside that everyone is going to leave us, that our doubt or questions will cause the plane of our faith we're riding on to go into a free fall.

And... it kind of will? But great news! You don't have to die in the crash. There's a parachute. You can jump. There's a soft landing. You can choose to trust that God isn't a tapestry to be unraveled. God is not a plane to be crashed. The tapestry was merely a depiction of your experience of God thus far. The plane crash is a bad dream you can wake up from. Pulling that thread will remove the adornments you've put upon God, the projections you've made about Love and Her purpose. Still, it will leave you with a clear picture of who you always were and an image of who you could be. The fearful dream is lifted when you perceive the Light correctly.

We are afraid, beloved, that if we are honest, and if we are seen for who we are, what we want, what we need, we are worried we will not be loved. But the opposite is true.

If people were to see who you honestly were, they would be healed by the Love that resides in you because Love is who you are. This may sound impossible, lofty, or backward to what your ego wants to tell you of what is possible. It might be different from your lived experience. But God's kin'dom is upside down, so roll with it. Love is the only truth, and our opinion of it does not change its status. (I don't make the rules here. Sorry, not sorry.)

These fears aren't unfounded, though, they are illusions. We learned from our experiences of faith that if we get real, if we are honest in a way that doesn't line up with what is expected of us, we will be abandoned. We must change and conform to be met with compassion. This is conditional love. It is a transaction. It is not real. But just because it is not real does not mean that it didn't hurt, but not for the reason we think.

On the surface, we think we are upset and hurt because someone hurt us. The Church hurt us. My pastor hurt me. My controlling fundamentalist partner. The "good Christian" health and wealth gospel.

But what truly hurts is the realization that we were living in a fantasy. What hurts is realizing we were worshiping an idol. Once we attained it, we recognize that the Jesus sold to us offers neither fulfillment nor healing, but another system of managing my fears by disavowing them and of mitigating my fear of God by managing my behavior.

What hurts is having our expectations not met in the way we desire. What hurts is traveling toward what you think is God, only to pull the curtain back on the Wizard of Oz to realize that it was a man and not a God, behind a curtain who has been scaring you into submission. What hurts is feeling powerless in the face of this grandest betrayal, to able to do nothing but feel the brute force of love lost and relational abandonment.

What hurts is feeling so stupid for believing that maybe you found a home only to find out it was built on sand. But we are not powerless. We are not alone. We are not stupid.

We were lied to. Again and again. Maybe they didn't know it was a lie, but regardless of who is to blame for said lie, the lie remains untrue. Yet for so long we afforded it reality, which makes it harder to change our minds, habits, and so on.

Many of us fell for the lie. But we know the truth now. We are starting to wake up. We're starting to ask the essential questions. We pulled back the curtain and saw the idol for what it was. Now that we've smashed the idol, we can build an Ebenezer[22] to mark for ourselves where we do not want to go again.

And how? How can we be honest about where God is leading us, how big our faith is growing? How can we start allowing truth to be the bedrock of our existence? By trusting that no matter what, when we are living honestly and act within our integrity, we can be healed. And when we are healed, the world will be healed.

Here's the thing, babe— when you live honestly, as completely who you are, fully loving yourself as God loves you, unwilling to compromise on your worth and the worth of others, it is likely it will upset someone (or multiple someone's) in your life. When a person who is in an unhealthy relationship dynamic begins to act in healthy ways, the unhealthy person(s) will do what they can to sabotage the progress being made because it is more comfortable to remain in unhealthy relational patterns than it is to face the pain we're ignoring. It is easier to stay in the illusion of something happy than to face the reality that things are dynamic and changing. It's easier to hold on than to let go.

Most of the time, they don't even realize that's what they are doing. It's part of the ego's job to keep us in our illusions, in our fantasies.

It's like the van image from the top part of the chapter. Mary starts to become who she is. She starts getting healed and begins to act in a way contrary to the norms of her community. And what happens next? She's thrown the in the back of a van for, you guessed it, an impromptu exorcism and Jesus' love being literally bashed against her body. It's a caricature of an example, but it's not far removed from so many of our realities. But what does Mary do?

Mary picks up the very thing that was thrown at her, the weapon formed against her, and says, "This is not a weapon." She is Christ in this moment, looking at the religious elite, looking at those who would seek to crucify her and declares that they don't know what they are doing. She doesn't

---

[22] An Ebenezer is an old word that means "a stone of remembrance." In the old testament, it was boundary makers and also altars that people would build in places to remember the great acts of God.

fight back. She breaks the cycle of violence with a declaration of truth and moves on.

Jesus tells us in the gospels that if a town does not receive you, shake the dust from your feet.

Perhaps it is time we began to shake the dust from our feet, fam. Maybe it's time we looked beyond the walls of the institutional Church, beyond the walls of our traditional family, beyond the walls of what's considered orthodox faith to find out what our faith is actually made of.

I am no longer interested in forcing my way into spaces that don't want me or my people or my friends. If a church sits ambivalent about marginalized folks, it sits on the side of oppression, and there it will reap the fruit of its sin. And at any time, they can choose to change, to repent for the forgiveness of their sin.

This is the miracle, y'all: we all have the choice to begin again.

We have the capacity to change. So, those of us who are having this grand awakening now must ask what we are willing to settle for. Are we willing to settle in pews in churches that aren't willing to hold all of us, all of our friends? Or will we shake the dust from our feet and go home, not settling for places that are below our divine, God-given worth?

There will be some who will want to stay in churches and fight within denominations for a seat at the table. That's dope and needed, but I don't believe that will be me anymore. It just isn't me. I'll shout against discrimination, naming it for the injustice that it is and advocating for clear policies in every church in America. Still, it is not worth my emotional energy any longer. I only have so much time on this planet. I'd rather spend it rejoicing in the family and joy I've found out here dancing in the desert than lamenting ad infinitum about what I've lost.

I once lost my life for the sake of the Gospel.

Then I found it in the Gospel. Just like He said I would.

...

The Bible says that when Jesus died on the cross, the veil that separated the part of the temple for everyone from the Holy of Holies, the place where they believed God's presence literally dwelt. I can imagine priests were horrified at what they saw. The Holy place was exposed to the profane. Those who were not worthy could look upon the dwelling of all worthiness.

If that did actually happen, I wonder what the onlookers must've thought, the ordinary people who were busy trying to survive under Roman oppression. They'd been told their whole lives, "This is where God lives." And then the veil was torn to reveal that there was no God there. Just a room with an altar.

Growing up, I was told that this was a sign that the Holy of Holies was now everywhere. This was a sign that the presence of God was now open to everyone through what Jesus did on the cross. But I'm not so sure this is the best reading of this because it implies that there was a separation in the first place.

What if the Holy was always everywhere?

What if the veil being torn exposed the illusion of separation instead of bridging some kind of gap?

What if the original sin was believing there was a separation at all?

What if the life of Jesus showed us what it looked like to live without that illusion of separation?

What if we could live like that?

This is belief is the one that saves me. Even when I don't feel it, even when I don't believe it, I am persuaded that neither height nor depth, nor angels nor demons, nor my ego, nor the church, nor my mental health, nor my sexuality, nor my gender, nor anything else in all creation, nor anything in the miscreation of my fearful mind, can separate me from the Love of God.

A famous painting by Andrei Rublev, depicting the Trinity, has a small rectangle in the actual table where the three angel-like figures are reclining, and it looks as though something is missing. One theory is that there was once a mirror there. This was to remind onlookers when they came upon the Godhead that they, too, were caught up in the divine dance of Love, in the mysterious movement we call God.

What if, when Dorothy pulled back the curtain at the end of the Wizard of Oz found not a man, but a mirror. What if she pulled back and she saw it was her all along?

I think the same can be true of those of us whose faith seems to be evolving or going up in flames. As you pull back the curtain of our faith, you will find a mirror. Slowly, it will occur to you that all the coincidences, all the good things that happened, all the things you are thankful for, it will occur to you that you had a hand in this. You are God's body. You are the conduit through which God experiences and interacts with the world. You are the Christ to the world in which you find yourself if you choose to be.

Back to that scene in the temple when the veil was torn. In some ways, those who were looking on did see a mirror. The tear shows us the truth that we are separated from nothing. At the same time, we are also confronted with the startling reality that we are worshiping a false idol, a belief system that can never satisfy our longing for that sense of home and wholeness we think we lack.

We have to forgive ourselves for our belief in something that couldn't heal us. And we have to forgive ourselves cause what the fuck else are we going to do! We didn't know any better. Beloved, there is good news.

When you forgive yourself for whatever it is that you think you did, you can gaze beyond the veil, into the holy of holies of your own Body and Soul, and gaze upon your reflection. Slowly, you'll realize that home can be found within you. The question you had about if there was more to life, more to God, more to this world– you will finally accept the fact that you weren't crazy.

You were right. You were right the entire time. You were right about everything. There *was* more to it all.

And the best part is now you get to experience it.

10
BLOOD SACRIFICE

Something my mama always tells me when I go out is, "be safe." I always reply, "I always am." Which is true. I really do try to be as safe as I possibly can. Depending on where I am going to be in my city for the day, I dress accordingly. Going downtown with bright red lips juxtaposed against a bright red beard may not exactly attract the right kind of attention. Honestly, I'd probably dress more femme than I do, but the south can be an unforgiving place when you don't fit neatly into the M or F on the intake form.

The first time a stranger accosted me, I was walking with my friend Jer in Denver. I fancied Jer at the time, and we were holding hands as we strolled toward some random coffee shop. We were talking about something, I can't remember what, and a loud voice from a passing car called out.

"Faggots!"

We both looked at each other like, "Did that dude just..." Yes. He did. I felt two things almost instantly. First, my knee-jerk reaction was anger. Who the hell does something like that? It was 2015 in Denver. Shouldn't we all be sharing a joint and not flinging slurs out of a car window?

Jer flipped that guy the bird, and we tried to recover what grace we had as we continued walking.

The second thing that registered is that this was the first time that I was visibly queer, the first time that someone could see me and point it out. The first time someone chose to verbally attack me for who I am. It was the first time I remember being scared as a queer person.

Images of Matthew Shepherd flooded my mind. Beaten face, tied to a fence, barely clinging to life. That could happen to me if I chose to be myself. Some people could look at me and merely assume my sexuality or gender. They could feel threatened by my mere existence and take out their insecurities on my body, for they cannot bring themselves to admit that I am merely an edifice for their soul. I'm but a lamb to be slaughtered because of the hate they feel towards their own iniquities.

I could be punished for their sin: the sin of believing they are separate me.

As I mulled this over with Jer, another emotion came up in my throat. It was pity. I honestly felt bad for that asshole who drove by.

How sad for you, you sweet bastard, that you can't experience the glory of who I am. You won't look hard enough. You won't inspect the light that shines in me, and therefore you will never get the revelation of how much light is in you.

I feel that way about every person who rejects queer people. This is not to discount the trauma and damage done to queer people in the name of religious conviction. That is real. I also believe that anytime we attack someone or something, we attack ourselves. The trauma goes in both directions. Often, the oppressor is so anesthetized to their own humanity. If they were in touch with their humanity, they would be able to see the humanity in the people that they hated and hurt and oppress. But they are distracted by the illusions of power.

In their belief that they are separate from me, they place themselves upon their various golden calves and declare each themself god. They believe it their divine right to exercise force over those who do not worship at their altar, to exact what they will from people and from the land in search of something which can only find when they finally are willing to face the suffering of their own existence:

Love. Forgiveness. Grace.

Standing there, in Denver, in the chilly thousand-foot elevation air, my anger and fear and sadness mixed like a cocktail. I asked myself what could be done. Is there any justice to be had? Was there any redemption to be had?

No. I would receive no apology. That dude will likely keep calling people fags as often as he jerks it to lesbian porn (which is statistically higher among Evangelical areas of the country where LGBTQ are most oppressed). What was there to do?

"Do you wanna get a drink?" Jer asked me. It was 1:30 PM. I was on vacation.

"Fuck yeah I do." With a cheers and some beers, I breathed in and reminded myself of who I was and what I had been set free from. I said a little prayer for the sad guy who called me and Jer faggots. I really do hope that he got free of his own shit and stopped hurting people. The rest of our day was a delight.

It was an era of progress. We just got gay marriage. Obama was still president. Queer Christians were popping out of the woodwork more and more every day. The future felt so hopeful. Neither one of us had any idea of how our lives would change next summer.

...

In the early morning of June 12, 2016, I was asleep in Washington, DC. My boss and I were there for Capitol Pride to sell some merch and meet some hot boys hopefully. This was my sixth or seventh pride festival that summer, so the routine was down pat by this point. Wake up. Fuel up. Roll out. Set up. Sell shit. Wrap up. Party hard.

The alarm went off. I was so freaking tired. Of course, I didn't sleep the night before because what is more important than being able to perform your work duties? Doing poppers at the club with a bunch of shirtless DC hotties, of course. My boss started talking almost instantly, which wasn't like them. Neither one of us had coffee yet.

"There was a shooting." To be honest, the first thing that went thru my head was a very sarcastic *"and?"*

I had grown up in a world where people got shot all the time. Columbine happened when I was in elementary school. Virginia Tech happened when I was in college. Sandyhook, too. I knew gun violence was a shitty thing. However, my preoccupation with trying to erase my sexuality all those years disallowed me from feeling the level of empathy needed to move me from complacency to action when it comes to being vocal about gun violence. I was so wrapped up in my own drama that I couldn't even care about the lives lost because of a completely preventable epidemic of violence.

"There were twenty-six people shot dead, and a bunch of others injured. It was at a gay club in Orlando."

The words hit my face and slid off like water on marble. I heard it. The data registered in my brain. My body froze. I don't know if I ever considered this a possibility. These bozos usually shot up malls and mosques and churches and synagogues and schools. Who the fuck would shoot up a gay club?

"Okay, we have to focus. We'll feel this later. We have a job to do."

I nodded, took a deep breath, and completely disassociated from my body and what He was feeling. Ex-gay therapy taught me how to do that really well.

As I got ready for the day, the news played in the background. Images of people lined up around the block to give blood. A climbing body-count. Details about the shooter. Details about the gun used. Information on the club. It was Latin night at Pulse. Stories about last words, last text messages, cries of outrage.

We load up the car, get to our location, set up, and wait for the festival to pick up. I hadn't cried yet. My smile was plastered on. My boss, on the other hand, was buried in their phone, looking at all the devastation. They kept slipping me details and hardly was functioning, in shock probably.

The day wrapped about seven hours later. We packed everything up into the car and returned, exhausted, to the hotel. As soon as we got back to our room, I dropped my shit, stripped, and stood under the hot water of the showerhead. The water pressure was phenomenal, I remember.

I sat down in the tub, water pouring directly on my head, legs held close to me as my silent sobs distorted my face into twisted anguish, my tears burning my eyes.

A voice was heard in Ramah. It was Rachel, mourning for her children because they were no more. She refused to be comforted.

I didn't want comfort. I wanted answers.

But I didn't want answers, though. I wanted justice.

But I didn't want justice, either. I wanted to feel safe.

But I didn't want to feel safe, either. I wanted to know that I was loved.

God, how could you let this happen? I had nothing and no one to direct my anger toward, not even God because this gaping hole that had been torn open in me felt void of love.

I thought back to my first club experience when I was nineteen. Smoky and dark and sketchy. I kissed a stranger and sweated through my clothes and had a hangover so massive that I swore off drinking then and there until the next time we wanted to dance.

As I reveled in that memory, the sounds of gunfire and screaming invaded my mind. In an instant, I was at Pulse. I was with the bodies lying on the ground. I was with the people trapped in the bathroom. I was aware, in no uncertain terms, that this could have been me. This could have been my friends.

It became clear that nowhere is safe for a queer body like mine. Not at home, not at church, and certainly not in public.

I open my eyes. The water is starting to get cold. My hands are beyond pruned, and I should probably let my boss use the shower. I pull on some comfy clothes and exit the bathroom.

The Tony Awards are on the television, and Hamilton is claiming every prize it's nominated for. It's not lost on anyone what happened, or how futile it felt to celebrate theatre and art in the face of tragedy. But really what else should one do in the face of tragedy and senseless violence but do something that will spark joy. My tears are gone by this point, but a part of me wanted so desperately to sob when I hear Lin Manuel-Miranda name the shooting and then give the iconic, "Because Love is Love is Love is Love..." speech.

Up on the rooftop, I watch the sunset over the DC skyline and start crying again, wondering how something could be so beautiful when something so awful happened less than twenty-four hours earlier. I call my mother and cry on the phone to her, and it sets in why she always tells me to be safe when I go out.

The immediate outpour of support from Christians was wild in the best and worst sense of the world. Some Christians celebrated that the dirty, sinful faggots had gotten mowed down. Some said that it was tragic, and they were praying for the LGBTQ community while still letting us know that homosexuality was a sin and that if we'd only repent.

It struck me that this was the first time that many Christians started seeing queer folks as human. Now that we could no longer be ignored, now that we were suffering in public, we could no longer be dismissed as a conjecture or lofty issue. But what hurt me more than conditional support and platitudinal prayers was the reality that these tributes were mostly meaningless.

How could you ever honor someone in death that you did not honor in life?

How could you offer comfort to those who lost someone when you damn those they lost to Hell?

Why is it that the world sees queerness as a threat? Why did this person, the shooter, feel like they had to take out their fear on my people? I couldn't help but hear every pastor on every pulpit I had ever seen growing up, talking about how the homosexual would be the death of America, the death of the Church if we didn't stand against it. Images of Pat Robertson on the television returned to me. I can still hear him blaming hurricane Katrina and 9/11 on queer folks, punishment for a nation who had tolerated the degenerates.

Then a memory of a guy who came to my last church and preached a sermon entitled "How to Raise Heterosexual Children." An ex-gay man who had two kids who were now elders at the church told us that the reason he titled the sermon this was because, "well, I've done it. I've successfully raised to straight kids." As if his performance had any bearing on his kids' sexuality. I felt so shitty after that, I went outside and just started bawling.

My pastor came up to me before I left and told me that he knew it'd be hard for me to hear, but he felt like I needed to experience that. I immediately left church that night and got blackout drunk with my fraternity brothers because I couldn't handle the grief of what that sermon did to me.

All these thoughts and memories flooded my head and my eyes as I drove home thirteen hours home to Atlanta from DC. I couldn't not go. I needed to be with my chosen family. A friend of mine opened his home open up to anyone who needed a place to go. We gathered to just be together, to process and cry. When I walked in the door, Myles saw me and pulled me deep into his arms, letting me fall apart while also signaling to someone to get me a beer.

That's a real friend, y'all.

...

We need to talk about numbers around guns real quick because maybe this is the first time you are hearing this. Perhaps you still don't see the connection between the public policy, the bad theology, and the dead bodies of people killed by gun violence.

So, let's get into it.

The United States is roughly 4% of the world's population. Funny enough, the US is also the world's largest arms dealer. This singular nation, my country, controls 31% of the world's global weapons market. The US supplies ninety-four other nations with the weapons their militaries use and supplies almost half of the other nations in the world with their weapons.

The US spends over $612 billion in defense. The second highest is Russia, which spends $76 billion. Now let those two different numbers sink in. That's a difference of $536 billion. The US spends more than the next ten countries on that list combined. We are a country that is continually preparing for war, instead of pouring that money into projects that engender peace.

And what about military bases? Many countries have bases in places outside of their formal borders to defend them and protect them and keep them safe. Russia has eight military bases in other countries, Great Britain has seven in other countries, and France has five in other countries. The United States, by contrast, has six-hundred and sixty-two military bases in different countries all over the world. That's apparently a conservative estimate. Some data suggests it might be as high as eight-hundred military bases because some information is classified.

So, the US sells more weapons, makes more weapons, owns more guns, brokers in more arms, spends more money on its own defense than any nation in the history of the world. Yet, what is wild to me is when conservative candidates running for office on a platform of strengthening the military. We're a military superpower. We can't be the most powerful because we already are, in terms of sheer military force. Furthermore, the Pentagon spends more on war and conflict than all fifty American states combined spend on health, education, welfare, and safety, and that is stuff you can just google.

In 2008, the year I graduated from high school, the Pentagon spent more money every five seconds that the average American earned that year. The Pentagon budget consumes 80% of individual tax revenue.

Now, let's get even more practical.

The US Military spends around $1 billion a year advertising to us. Somewhere in the neighborhood of $6 million gets paid professional sports teams to have moments where the military are honored. That's not just something they do out of love for the troops. They're getting cash for that. The NFL, the NBA, the NHL, major league baseball, and soccer teams are all paid by the military to honor soldiers. So, all those moving moments we see on television and at big sporting events, and it is indeed moving, remember that. The military paid for that moment to happen, and they are paying with money that comes from taxes. So really, you helped pay for that moment. If you've ever seen a military commercial online or on TV, you, as a taxpayer, also helped pay for those US military ads that were advertising to you about the US military.

Switching gears –Nuclear bombs are a thing.

The current estimate is it would take one hundred nuclear bombs to block out the sun, to change the climate, to decimate the environment, and basically make the world an uninhabitable, Mad Max: Fury Road-esque wasteland. Only nine countries out of 196 countries in the world have nuclear weapons. Between these nine countries, they possess just over *16,000* nuclear bombs. 93% of those sixteen-thousand nuclear bombs are owned by the US and Russia.

Shocker, right? (Just kidding.)

That means the US, alone, has *7,300* nuclear bombs.

One hundred nuclear bombs will make the earth a wasteland, and the United States has *7,300* of them...I *really* want that to sink in. Because is that not terrifying?

Only two of these bombs have ever been used in the history of the world. It was when the US dropped two atomic bombs on Hiroshima and Nagasaki.

8,000 people died instantly in Hiroshima, a body count that grew to more than 192,000 over the following days due to radiation and, ya know, general destruction of their city. That second number wasn't released until the 50th anniversary of the bombing.

Over 7,000 people died instantly when the second bomb was dropped on Nagasaki. That's over 343,000 people dead in a matter of seven days from two weapons of mass destruction.

Our government did that.

Now let's get personal.

The US is 4% of the world's population and owns somewhere between 40-50% of the world's privately-owned guns. Some estimates are 270 million non-military guns are owned by civilians. Some say it could be closer to 300 million non-military guns. But we don't know that because the way we track who owns, who buys, and how sells firearms in this country is entirely outdated and favors the sales of gun companies over the safety of people.

The second-highest gun ownership is in ownership, which has 46 million guns, is India. However, India makes up 1.2 billion people, 17% of the world's population, so it's a bit more proportional.

The country with the highest homicide by gun rate is America, 68% of all US homicides, in fact. Those estimates mean that there are between 90, and 112 guns per hundred people. The country with the second-highest rate of gun related deaths is Serbia, at sixty-nine guns per hundred, and then Yemen, a war-torn nation in turmoil right now at just fifty guns per hundred people.

This one nation, our nation, 4% of the world's population, has more guns than any other country on earth. Our government spends more money on guns than any other nation, sells more weapons to more nations than any other nation in the history of humanity, spends billions on advertising it's military to its own citizens, is the only nation who has ever dropped a nuclear bomb, and it did it twice. This nation is also the nation that has the most shootings of any nation mass shootings on the face of the planet, accounts for 31% of shootings between 1966 and 2012.

This is our country. This is the United States of America, and we have a gun problem, a weapons problem, a violence problem.

And what does it all have to do with the church? Or faith? Or bad theology?

Everything.

Studies show that the majority of Americans across the political spectrum want common-sense gun reform, which consists, among other things, of mandatory background checks for anyone buying a gun, a ban on military assault rifles, closing loopholes in the law for selling weapons outside of regulated processes so that people who shouldn't have guns won't have them.

The lie which has been propagated, and that the evangelical church has bought, is "the liberals" want to take your guns. This is not the case. We're not out to take your permit held gun away, or your hunting rifles away. We just want simple things that could stop our friends, our parents, our family, and our kids from dying. We want to send our children to high school and not worry that someone might kill them. We want to go to a concert and not have to worry so much about where the emergency exit is if bullets start flying.

It is shocking to me that I, an older millennial, have lived with gun violence in schools since I was in middle school when Columbine happened. You'd think that one act of violence would make us rethink what we did. But then another one happened. And another. And then it wasn't just in high schools, but colleges, and then in theaters, at night clubs, at concerts, at churches and mosques and synagogues, at elementary schools.

Think about Sandyhook Elementary! Does anyone remember that? Babies! Gun violence took our babies, and the conservative, Christian-family values republicans still took money from the NRA. The NRA only has one interest: keeping their sales up, not protecting people. And those same conservative, Christian family values republicans did nothing. Christians didn't vote them out of office, so by proxy, we are part of the problem.

Gun violence is a spiritual issue. It is as old as our history, which began in violence. It is a sin issue.

When I read the words of Jesus, I hear one who preaches we are to love our enemies. This conflicts with the doctrine of American superiority that would say that the individual right to own machines that are meant for one purpose, to kill, is more important than the good of everyone. It conflicts with the prophetic words that in the kingdom of God, spears will be beaten into plowshares. Weapons will be destroyed. On top of that, it plays right along with the themes of the Old Testament that show what can happen when a nation amasses power like the US has. It shows us how being a war profiteer leads to moral decay and the downfall of a nation.

I don't know about you, but I am a Jesus follower, and to the best of my knowledge, the prince of peace doesn't carry a gun. And at minimum, I think he'd be in favor of common sense gun reform so less people died and less people got rich from those people dying.

…

In 2016 when Donald Trump was elected as the 45th president of the United States, I was fucking floored. The night he was elected, me and my homies gathered in a tiny apartment, were doing pickle backs (whiskey chased by pickle juice (it's delicious, don't hate)), and getting ready to crown Hillary as our queen for the people. But you know what they say about assuming things right?

Makes you a democrat on November 4, 2016.

The night went on and people trickled out as a caricature nightmare became a fully enfleshed reality. This man who ran on a platform of xenophobia, who called Mexicans rapists, who couldn't actually articulate any policy beyond making our country great again, had won. And we knew it was going to be bad, but holy shit, y'all… what a fucking wild four years.

If you lived during 2020 as the rise of the worst global pandemic, COVID-19, there is no way the blinders weren't a little removed for you. We were all affected. There is not a way you didn't notice the massive groundswell of support for the Black Lives Matter movement. There's no way you didn't hear of George Floyd, killed by a police officer when that officer knelt on his neck even after he became unresponsive. The world saw it play out on a cell phone camera video.

There's no way you didn't see the billboards that Oprah put up around the country to tell the story of Breonna Taylor, who was killed in her bed when police broke into her house announced on an unrelated issue, and fired their guns, killing her. None of the officers were charged with her murder, though one was charged for the bullet that hit the wall in the adjacent apartment.

Daniel Purdue was having a mental health episode when police put a spit hood over him, causing him to be unable to breathe. He died later in police custody from asphyxiation.

Rayshard Brooks fell asleep in the line at a Wendy's drive-thru in Atlanta, GA and when police arrived, they escalated the issue, resulting in Rayshard being shot twice in the back when he tried to get away from them.

And those are just the names of the people who made into the headlines. These stories are the rule, not the exception, to how policing has affected communities of color, especially Black people in the US. They died for sleeping in their own bed, for having mental health issues, for falling asleep in the car, for allegedly using a counterfeit $20. Tell me, beloved, do you think you should be killed for that? Do you think *anyone* should die for things like this?

What if someone stole something, then? Or what if they were selling single cigarettes or their mix tape? Or what if you get stopped at a traffic light, should you end up inexplicably dead in a jail cell later like Sandra Bland did?

The issue is not that there are one or two bad cops on a handful of forces, but that there is a system and a cultural that allows for police to use lethal force with little to no consequences. They are here to "help us" or that is what they tell us. But what the numbers tell us is that increased police presence does not decrease crime or violence. They simply catch more folks in the neighborhoods that are policed more. Those neighborhoods are invariably Black neighborhoods with a police force that doesn't live among or understand the community they are sworn to protect.

And it makes a lot of sense when you know where the police as an institution comes from, and it wasn't some necessity to protect society. The police originated from the slave catchers from right near the Civil War era. They were tasked with rounding up formerly enslaved Black folks who ran away from their captors. And as America evolved, these slave catchers evolved into the police we know, enforcing Jim Crow era restrictions on Black folks, allowing and often perpetuating violence against them.

Why didn't we learn that in elementary school? Why did anti-racism training end with Dr. Martin Luther King, Jr.'s dream and the vision of everyone being equal without actually living into that dream? Society has white King's work as a demure pastor but he was killed because he said he wanted white folks and Black folks to hold hands. He was shot because he said we should be judged by the content of our character no the color of our skin. He was assassinated because he dared challenge the world's violent imagination and say, "another way is possible."

Friends, whether this is your first foray into talking about racial justice, police violence against Black and Brown bodies, guns, the military, or anything else we've covered here, or whether this is old hat for you, the reality is that right now Black folks are dying at the hands of cops, because of poverty, because of preventable reasons, due to a systemic issue that began when European colonizers stole Africans from their home and forced them here.

There are no bootstraps too pull yourself up by when you were naked when you came off the ship. There are success stories out there of amazing Black folks who are making their way in the world. Damn, we even had a Black president for a little bit. But this country isn't equal. Never has been, because Black folks were kept in slavery for 339 years, followed by 89 of domestic terrorism during Jim Crow, and in 1954 they got the right to vote. That's over 400 years of outright oppression and forced servitude, followed by the past seventy years of color blindness, leading white folks in power to largely ignore the issues Black communities face because it does not affect them.

This has to change.

In the year 2020, we've heard the call to defund the police and redirect that money into community programs that will actually benefit people, getting them what they need rather than having an untrained police officer come in to deal with a situation they are not trained for. Why not have a therapist or a social worker come to an emergency suicide call? Why not have a people's advocate talk to the person sleeping on the bench, getting them a place to stay and food, not arrest them for being poor? Why not give the resources to the community to help get them out of the issues that are causing them to turn to crime rather than punishing them for doing what they must to survive?

It seems simple, and that's because it is. It's a simple problem with complicated path because someone will inevitably say, "Not all cops are bad." "I know a police person and their gay and black!" "My mom's a police woman and she loves her community."

Great. I love that your person is an exception to the rule of violence that most prevalent in the policing industrial complex. But I'm not talking about those people. We're not talking the few good eggs, we're talking about the majority of the eggs who are rotten to the core. We are talking about all the people that your one good egg failed to stop. We are discussing the policeman who knelt on George Floyd's neck till he died. We are talking about the cops who busted down a door and killed Breonna Taylor in her bed, facing no consequences.

Your friend, your parent, your whoever who you love in the police is not enough to stop the violence. And unless they are willing to stand up in their department to make changes, unless they are willing to ruffle feathers to get the justice we are crying for, I contend that they are part of the problem, and you are complicit by proximity if you can't call them on it.

This violence been happening so long that we think this is normal. And it doesn't have to be. Not anymore.

...

We have to look at the data. We can no longer ignore what the facts are telling us about gun violence in the United States. How many more high schools will be shot up before we are moved to elect people who can help stop this? How many more black bodies will pile up before we hold police accountable for the damage they've done and still do to the black community? How many concert venues, elementary schools, clubs will have blood on the floor before we tell those in power that their time is done?

I can hear in my mind already, a Christian reading this and getting offended. "But I didn't pull the trigger." "I've never been mean to a gay person." "I've got black friends." "What does this have to do with theology or faith?"

Again, everything.

If you saw me, a queer person, as your family, as your beloved sibling, as worthy of protection, you would protect me. If you really did care about me, you would do something about the things that threaten my existence, and your own. If this epidemic of preventable gun violence has shown us anything, is that you can be praying in any house of worship, including a church, and still get shot. Why wouldn't you want to do everything in your power to protect your church, your family, your people? Honestly, make it make sense to me why you wouldn't want that.

The reality is many don't see me as family. They do not see me as worthy of protection. They live in fear and can only imagine a world in which they can keep themself safe because safety is scarce, and safety for me means they will not be safe. In a way, this is true. To stand in solidarity with marginalized people is to accept the consequences of being in proximity to those who are despised.

I am seen as separate; therefore, I am expendable. If I get killed, no big deal. And that may seem hyperbolic, but that's really what it boils down to. Any theology that fails to affirm queer people transforms them in the minds of those who hold this theology into the other. And if I am separate from you, if you don't have to experience my pain, it doesn't matter to you.

That collective rejection of queer persons manifests itself in policies that keep us from using the bathroom, keep us from lifesaving healthcare, and in fear of people who hate us so much that they open fire in the wee hours of the morning on Latin night at a gay club.

It's bad theology. It's all connected.

And it's killing all of us.

11
LET IT BURN

My friend Emily has this incredible poem where she talks about how she never lost her faith. She compares it all to a forest fire and the very last line in her performance, she raises her hand and says, "I didn't lose my faith. It burned. Right. Up." Snap. Silence.

Then the room remembers to breathe after having the air sucked out of our lungs by a poem about holy fire. Damn.

The whole poem is a prayer request in which she asks the Fire to burn away everything that isn't going to last. Burn my faith to the ground whatever is supposed to spring forth out of it can. Let me be stripped of what isn't You, God, everything that isn't Love, anything that will not heal. Let the illusions pass away and let me be at one with You.

It reminds me of the story of Jesus wandering and fasting in the desert for forty days. He's just been baptized and had the Holy Spirit land on him like a dove and the voice of God saying, "This is my Son, in Him, I am well pleased." People always point out that this was before Jesus had begun his earthly ministry. Before He was an enemy of the state and a heretic and a revolutionary and *that* Jesus, God was pleased with Him.

The waters of baptism are nothing magical, though they are sacred. As an Evangelical and semi-Baptist, we got baptized when we were around ten or so. I don't know why that was. Maybe because by that age, we were all responsible for chores? Or perhaps it was because puberty was hitting, and we were expected to be young men and women. And to be a man or woman of any sort of honor included being a part of the Church. Much past thirteen

163

years of age, you'd start to raise a suspicious eyebrow of the other parents and maybe your youth pastor. If you hit sixteen and you still hadn't walked down the aisle at the altar call, you were practically in open rebellion.

Like I told you earlier, my experience of the Spirit was quite powerful. I was honestly hoping that the giant baptismal bathtub, with its giant crucifix affixed overhead, would give me a similar experience. But much to my chagrin, when the youth pastor put me under and brought me up, nothing happened. People clapped. I smiled. I moved out of the water as the congregation sang the refrain.

Now I belong to Jesus, Jesus belongs to me,

Not for the years of time alone, but for eternity.

I was confused. My mind spun with questions.

"Wait... wait, that's it? That's what people cry about? Wasn't... was I supposed to feel something?" I remember, standing sopping wet in the storage room behind the baptismal tub, wondering if I had done it wrong. But I couldn't think about it for too long. Mom told me we were going to the Mexican restaurant to celebrate my soul being saved from eternal damnation. (She didn't phrase it that way. She just said, "baptism," but let's be honest.)

What was baptism for my community of Evangelicals? It was fire insurance. It was the way you proved you believed in Jesus. That was really it. That was how you "got saved." But my suspicion now was that I got saved way before I came up from my watery grave. And maybe even before I walked down the aisle and confessed my belief in Jesus. And perhaps even before I was knit together in my mother's womb.

If there is no Hell to be saved from, perhaps I have always been saved. Maybe I have always been safe.

So, what is the point of the baptism? What was the point of Jesus being baptized by his cousin, John?

There are symbols upon symbols and volumes of poetry we could, but I want to hone in on the idea that comes to us from our mainline siblings who practice infant baptism. Growing up, I was told that it was sinful to baptize a baby. Babies couldn't actively choose to embrace the grace of Jesus,

and thus the infant baptism was invalid. How joyful I was to learn that this was not what it was at all.

To baptize a child is to say, "You are part of the Beloved of God. You belong. You are loved. You are indeed a Child of Love. And the promises of eternal life and everlasting love are for you, as well." It is affirming the promises of God for them and over them. It is, in some ways, a parent saying, "I understand that this child is both mine and also not mine, for they belong to God and to themself."

What if this is what Jesus was doing at the Jordan? What if Jesus stepping into the baptismal waters was to say, "I affirm the promises of God for myself. I submerge myself in the flow of the Spirit. I arise to affirm my communion with All." And then, in a very light Divine flex, the Holy manifests Herself to say, "This is my Son." (Just as a fun exercise in imagination, what if that voice was the voice of a woman?)

What if Jesus was showing us what it is to accept the truth about ourselves by accepting the truth about himself? What if Jesus is saying, "Yes, I know I am part of the Beloved, and the Beloved is a part of me." What if, in those same baptismal waters, we were saying the same thing. What if we heard God's voice speaking over us the promises of our baptism, of our status as Beloved children of God?

What if it was that simple?

I think it is.

At the same time, this concept is seemingly impossible to accept perfectly in every moment. Thankfully, Grace is not presupposed on my ability to accept it, nor even on my own belief in its possibility. It continues to exist as the river flowing in front of me. It is whether I choose to put myself in the water, to baptize myself in it. When I am willing to accept it for myself, I can hear clearly God's voice.

How often do we hear God's voice, and then become driven into the desert by the Holy Spirit? (Did you think I forgot about that? Don't worry, it's coming around to a point.)

So, Jesus gets a huge confidence boost from Sky Daddy. He then finds himself facing off with the *literal* Devil who decides to attack the thing that God had just spoken over Jesus, his identity.

"If you really are the Son of God..."

Now, I've got to confess here and now that I don't believe in a literal, anthropomorphized Satan the same way I don't believe in literal Hell as a place. There's a whole interesting discussion of how Satan shows up throughout the Bible that shows that he is more of a literary device than an actual demonic force in the universe coming against us. Still, we can talk about that later if you want. However, I do think Jesus was tempted by the devil. I think Jesus, being human, probably had all the same doubts we did.

I imagine Jesus wandering, wondering, questioning. "Am I really the guy for this? Am I really who they say I am? Am I even up for this? Will they receive it? What if this gets me killed? What if I lose my family? Who is even going to listen to what I have to say?" Even after having his identity spoken over Him as Son of God, he doubts. He is open to the questions, and the questions bring about some startling things.

Satan tempts Him with turning rocks into bread, with power and influence, and even with the sweet release of death. But Jesus says no, and not just because He could combat it with His knowledge of scripture as an old pastor always taught me from the pulpit. Jesus rejects these things because He knows they are illusions. Rather than giving himself to an illusion, He returns to Himself, to the call God has placed on Him.

He makes room for the questions, the doubts, and as soon as He releases Himself back to the truth of who He is, and that perhaps it is okay to have questions without always answering them, the text says the devil flees Him, that angels attend to Him. They were always waiting for Him. As soon as Jesus was ready, He received.

Jesus in the desert, being tempted by the power-filled allure of certainty, being tortured by thoughts of fear, still allowed Himself to be healed. He agreed with God, and it sent Him on His path. I wonder if Jesus going through the desert was necessary. If Jesus had truly accepted who He was at His baptism, if He believed and agreed with God, would Jesus have needed to go through that dark night of the soul for forty days?

Perhaps, but how wonderful to know that Jesus, our brother, has also been where many of us wander now. Jesus went into the desert place to be stripped of everything that was not Love, everything that wasn't necessary, everything that was an illusion, everything that wasn't God that He might be one with God in everything He did. He was accepting the reality of His own union with God for the first time. It is from His experience of God that Jesus then begins to tell others, to call others to this better way of practicing faith and doing life.

I imagine that Jesus, having grown up in an oppressed and occupied land, under a culture that was desperately trying to cling to their heritage through a rigorous practice of faith, I wonder if He felt bad or weird about owning His newfound faith and practice. Did He have guilt the same way I do, a sense that I might be betraying my people? Or at least betraying those who I perceived were my people. I wonder if in the heat of the desert if the faith of Jesus burned right up.

...

I think Jesus was exactly who He said He was. I really *do* believe in some weird way that's beyond my comprehension that Jesus was the Holy incarnate. The Bahá'í faith names Jesus as one of the Holy manifestations among many in an eternal line of holy teachers. I believe He was a manifestation of the Divine. I think He still *is* a manifestation of the Divine.

I do not believe the Holy stopped incarnating Herself after Jesus. I know She was becoming incarnate far before whispers of virgin births, before hints of resurrection, before whispers of death even. The whole universe is the Cosmic Mother incarnate, a product of Her desire.

It is said that Jesus appeared to five-hundred disciples at once. I spent my entire life just accepting that as just some random fact in my Rolodex of useless Bible trivia until I actually read that statement and realized how ridiculous it sounded. Jesus appeared to five-hundred disciples at once... excuse me? That's fucking wild. As someone who is *trying* to be a good #BiblicalChristian, I could totally believe that.

Then Jesus apparently came to Paul and blinded him on the side of the road for a few days. And then he just accepts it and follows it? Listen, I don't like a lot of Paul's writing, but his testimony? I wouldn't say it's the wildest thing people have claimed to believe. No wilder than a man who got executed, buried, and then, whoopsie his body is gone. Jk! Here He is, do you wanna touch his flesh wounds? (Also, eww gross.)

What if Jesus was still appearing to us today? The version of myself that has my feet firmly planted on the earth would point to the ethereal truth of the Christ being reborn in us every time we choose to return to Love. The mystic wacko incarnated being part of me wholeheartedly believes Jesus is still with us. Appearing to us. Talking to us. Guiding us. Jesus shows us what is possible for those who surrender to the reality of our limitless union with God.

I believe Jesus is my brother, my spiritual ancestor, and my teacher. *A Course in Miracles* tells us that Jesus had his mind entirely healed by the Holy Spirit and understood fully His union with All. Because Jesus did this in His humanity, it shows us what we are all capable of as children of God, co-heirs with Christ. We can be healed. We can start revolutions. We can learn to forgive ourselves.

I love Jesus. And I will follow Him where He leads me. Even if that is away from the Church. Even if that is away from the label of Christian all together, if that's what it takes.

...

The first time I heard the voice of God was at age sixteen. I was at one of those weird youth retreat things, and one activity was asking God to speak to us and to listen for God. They shared the story from the 1 Samuel when Sammy keeps hearing God call to him, but he thinks it's Eli, his teacher, calling. And then Eli finally gets it. Samuel hears the voice of YHVH[23]. He instructs Samuel to say, "Speak Lord, your servant hears."

So, next time Samuel gets woken up by the voice, he speaks the words, and then God tells him, "See, I am about to do something in Israel that will make both ears of anyone who hears of it tingle." First of all, what a line, right? It's gonna make your ears tingle when you hear this divine tea, mama. Both ears!

He goes on to tell Samuel that Eli is about to get his ass handed to him because his kids were blaspheming God. Eli apparently didn't do anything to stop it. He knew about something that he could have prevented. He could have done the right thing, and he didn't. So, he was punished by his sins.

Samuel told Eli everything God told him about the iniquities that Eli apparently knew about (Aka - Eli had done some shit and knew he done wrong). And Eli said, "Yup. That's the Lord. God will do whatever he sees as right."

Basically, "may I be dealt with however I'm supposed to be dealt with." The text goes on to say that Samuel's words never fell to the ground, meaning

---

[23] YHVW is the English transliteration of the Tetragramaton, the ancient Hebrew rendering of the unspeakable name for God.

he called it like he saw it, and as God showed him, and he was right. This passage shows us what a prophet does: they name the thing for what it is, and they are right. Their words don't fall to the ground. What they say stands up to the weight of scrutiny.

Today, there is an established church full of false prophets claiming to hear the voice of God, claiming to follow Jesus, but what they say isn't true. Their words fall to the ground.

They say, "We care about *insert your cause here.*" "We welcome *insert your marginalized identity here.*" But they demonstrate that they care but for one thing, and that is the comfort of an illusion. They show that their welcome is conditional, and their affection is used as a bargaining chip instead of a meal to be shared. Their words fall to the ground. That isn't Love. That isn't God.

I've met prophets. They don't look like the preachers I listened to growing up. They are black and queer and fat. They are native and transgender and woman. They are Buddhist and Witch and Bahá'í and Athiest. And yes, many of them are Christians, but many wouldn't call them that. They are not perfect, but saints never are. That isn't a requirement. Willingness is.

Willingness to listen for God. Willing to listen *to* God. Willingness to ask more questions. Willingness to share what God is saying to them. Willingness to make the space inside their heart even bigger for the sake of more Love. Willingness to try. Willingness to do the next right thing. Willingness to be wrong. Some of these prophets call Jesus friend, some call him Lord, some don't call Jesus anything.

I know they are all prophets because they are naming the reality of what is happening right now. They recognize the illusions for what they are and speak so that others may perceive them too. They speak, and we know what they say is true. They name the consequences for persisting in our sin, and their words do not fall to the ground.

What I see in this story of Samuel's early days is a cautionary tale of what it is to blindly trust those who would exercise spiritual authority over others simply because they claimed some perceived moral high ground. In this story, I hear God giving us a clear example of how simple it can be to hear from God and trust it.

In this, I see a path forward for so many of us.

We have to believe that we could actually hear from God. And maybe not just that we could, but that we actually are hearing from God in real-time. Some of it will be in writing, some of it will be in stories, some of it in religion. Still, there are those of us who will see our lives as a holy text, a story as valid and real as anything we might read in the Bible. We will be still, listen, hear God, and respond with, "Speak Lord, your servant hears you."

Our dear sister, Rachel Held Evans, said in her last book that what she "loved about the Bible is the story isn't over. There are still prophets in our midst. There are still dragons and beasts." And she was right. The story of the Bible can't be over. God can't be contained in just sixty-six books. God can't be contained in only one religious tradition.

Beloved, we must actually listen to God's voice. You know it because it feels like peace. It looks like love. It sounds like life. And perhaps you'll know the voice of God because maybe, just maybe, both your ears will tingle when you hear it.

...

There are stories throughout the Christian tradition of the saints having encounters with the saints who came before them, with Jesus himself, and Mary, and the Archangels. Many of them reported experiencing miracles or being a conduit through which miracles occurred. These stories range from the mundane to the fantastical. But it is not an experience of miracles that truly blows us away about the saints of cannon. Miracles are just naturally occurring instances, which are extensions of love. What captivates us is how their lives were transformed to be more loving, more selfless, more like what we assume God to be like.

They are our siblings. They give us examples of what it is to hear from God, showing us that it is possible to hear from God outside of formerly established channels, and even though some channels the establishment would deem unholy and heretical. Yet, nothing could stop them in their pursuit of God. They kept going. They kept doing the thing God was leading them to do, saying the things God was whispering in their ears.

And so it is with us. I believe we are in the midst of another great awakening, but beyond anything we thought was possible. We are hearing the voices of prophets of old joined by prophets of today, calling for a return to Love.

So often, our experiences of God are discredited because we've given power to a Church that seeks to dictate what is valid and invalid. Once again, the process of our awakening and liberation includes divesting power from illusion and returning it to our bodies, giving validation to our experiences of God without qualification.

Let me say that another way.

I don't give a flying fuck if anyone believes me anymore. I don't care if people call me a Christian. I don't care if people call me a false prophet because I chose to love myself and others more and declared anything in the way of that Love as sin. I don't care if my practices move me to a place that is beyond the boundaries of what it means to be a Christian, because those aren't boundaries God created anyways. God didn't even make the Church! We did. So, even if the Church passes away, and it will, I still believe the Word of God will stand forever. (And I don't mean the Bible.)

...

Back to that story about when I heard God's voice for the first time.

I was sixteen. I'm sitting there. Praying. "Speak Lord, your servant hears you." I just heard, clear as a bell, a voice very much like my own, but also, not my own.

"If you do not speak, they will never know."

It hit me in my chest and radiated outward, shaking my whole body. I looked around, wondering if anyone else felt that. I asked my friend, he said he got nothing. But I heard something.

I had no clue what it meant or if I actually heard it, but I believe I heard that sentence, and it's been something I keep coming back to in my own life. If I don't speak, if I don't open my mouth and say the things that I am here to say, other people might not know.

If I don't speak, if I don't tell the truth about what is happening to me and my faith, if I can't be honest, I will be misunderstood.

If I don't speak, if I don't convey the fact that I was once trapped by rule and dogma and now I am free, someone might think it's impossible to be free in this life.

God is writing a gospel story with every single one of our lives. A story of liberation and strife and big dreams and beauty and great sadness and survival and magic and mystery and endless possibility.

It was a story that was meant to be filled with joy that overflows and peace that passes understanding. There are ways to get there, ways to move from the sense of separation that we think is there to the knowledge that we were always one with Love. Some of it, at least for me, doesn't look like what fundamentalist version of me from my past would call "Christian."

I don't worry about that anymore. Jesus wasn't even a Christian, so I'm okay, I think.

...

I had an epiphany the other day as I sat in the coworking space, finishing this book.

I was under the impression that I was going to write a book that was going to help people hold on to their faith by rejecting bad theology. I hope that is what I've accomplished. Still, the epiphany I came to is that his book came through me so that I might rid myself of my own illusions that I am separated from Love. I wrote this book because I needed to finally give myself permission to leave behind what no longer serves me. In some ways, I think I've always known what I believed. I just need to figure out why I believed what I did.

The Church handed me all the tools. It gave me a tradition and a language and a framework to work within, and in many ways, it still gives me so much. It's a rich tradition with so much good stuff baked in. But unfortunately, it is not the beauty of Jesus' teachings that have made the most significant impact on the world. Empire quickly took something that was a fringe religion and turned it into a tool of hegemony. Frankly, it's been fucking a lot of shit up ever since.

So, do we remain? Do we try to reclaim and reform something that could be so beautiful? Or do we begin again? Do we begin to find new ways of connecting with God? Do we continue to follow Jesus through our deserts?

John the Baptist told us that the one who would come after him would baptize us with fire. And maybe that is true. Perhaps the Church is burning, and rather than running for the doors, we've got our eyes closed, hands up, worshiping a melting image of Jesus on a crucifix, not realizing *He is not here.*

I'll admit, that sounds like a very fatalist view of the Church. But given our track record, I'm just not that confident. I'd love to be wrong, though. I desperately want to be wrong.

Weirdly enough, I don't think I'm going to stop going to my little Baptist church here in Atlanta. They are the Christ to me. They center a brown, immigrant, radical Jesus, and it's embodied in the congregation, in our lifestyles, our values, and our collective action. That's organized religion organizing around the right thing. I love it. I want my little church to survive and thrive, but I wouldn't be too sad if we closed. We'd keep doing our work, keep trying to love well, keep showing up for one another, and showing up for protests. And we'd still keep singing karaoke on Wednesdays, where the sacraments are good weed and dark beer.

We'd keep following Jesus, whatever that means.

I wrote this book because I needed to rise from my own ashes. I needed to grow. I needed to be able to say, without feeling afraid, knowing that my place in God's heart is never in question, that I love Jesus so much, but I just don't know if I'm a Christian. But I suppose it doesn't matter what I think, does it? Because what does the word Christian even really mean? There is no universal way to be Christian anymore there than there is a universal way to be human.

The reality is that only one question matters when it comes to identifying myself, and it is this:

Who do you say that I am?

ACKNOWLEDGEMENTS

As I sit here writing these acknowledgements, I'm overcome with gratitude to every single person who has said, "Your work has helped me." I'm so glad, and I'm grateful for every kind word, prayer, positive vibe, and loving thought you've sent me.

I have to give thanks for the following humans who helped me achieve this goal of getting this damn book finished!

In no particular order...

To my Mom. Thank you for changing your mind. Thank you for showing up for me. Thank you for loving me no matter what. You have no idea how rare it can be for a child to have a parent like you. I love you. And I know you hate cuss words but thanks for loving me despite my potty mouth.

To my best friend, Myles Markham. Thank you for saying yes to a random email from a desperate missionary. That one yes changed my life. I love you, and I'll be forever grateful for our friendship.

To my best friend, Jon Gilpatrick. I've never been afraid to be myself around you. I love how you always remind me of how capable I am, and that you're always down for stupid fun. I love you. Thank you for helping me realize my potential.

To my sister, Sarah Heath. You saw this coming back under the beer tent at Goose. I've got you to thank for spurring me on. You were the first person who told me I didn't have to fight for people who didn't love me well while also showing me what chosen family could be. I love you. And I can't wait to be neighbors.

To my brother, Matthias Roberts. We fucking did it, mate. I'm so proud of us. Thank you for being a source of accountability, encouragement, and kindness. You remind me that I'm not as much of a bad ass as I think I am, and that I, in fact, do need other people. I love you. Let's go on a trip this year, okay? I think we deserve.

To my sister, Jamie Lee Finch. You gave me the privilege of going second. Your willingness to give advice, to encourage, and to celebrate my wins as your own speaks volumes to your character. Thank you for giving me the courage to flip the bird to those who won't understand and just do the damn thing. I love you. Let's do more witchy shit.

To my brother, Mike McHargue. I would never have imagined that sharing two beers in the sticky summer air would have led to the friendship we have now. I'm so grateful for your work. But moreover, I'm grateful for how you've never ever made me feel like I didn't belong. I love you. I can't wait for more adventures.

To my sister and mentor, Micky ScottBey Jones. I have learned so much from you. Your words and your actions continue to remind me that to choose hope, to practice forgiveness, and to stay open even when we are hurt... it is the only way we can heal. You are a grace in my life. I'm grateful for the ways you've brought me in and made me your brother. I freaking love you. See you at the Silent Disco, High Priestess of the Twerk. 🎩

To our dear sister, Rachel Held Evans. Before this book came into this iteration, you told me, "You've got this." I hear your voice, even now, encouraging me to keep going. Thank you for your support of my career, my writing, and my community. I love you and I miss you, we all do. And I know that you are still with all of us.

To my editor, Kit Kennedy. I am so thankful that you reached out to me and encouraged me to self-publish literal *years* ago. I had never dreamed I could pull this off, but you saw it! And I'm so glad you did. I know I couldn't have pulled it off without your keen eye. Spirit knew what She was doing when we got connected. Can't wait for more future collaborations.

To my brother and sometimes pastor, Daniel Bass. I'm so glad we met on the worst day of our lives. I couldn't have imagined thriving the way we are now. Your integrity inspires me to keep my own. Blessed am I for finding a friend as honest and kind as you. I love you. Also, I'm for real about that marriage pact. 40 is gonna be here before we know it, so lmk if ur down.

To my internet cousins and #faithfullyLGBT fam. I'm never not amazed by us. Never forget what we have survived to be here. We are strong as hell. And we will heal ourselves so that we can heal the world. Remember to be kind to one another and be gentle with yourself. Thank you for your support of my work since that first blog to the present moment. Thank you for teaching me.

And to an assortment of lovely folks who have encouraged me in one way or another, helped me, promoted me, given me space, cried with me, inspired me, and generally have helped make this huge ass step in my work... Michael Gungor, Lisa Gungor, Austin Channing Brown, Rev. Nadia Bolz-Webber, Rev. Jaqcui Lewis, Rev. Jes Kast, Rachel Kurtz, the Hedge of Protection, Corey Pigg, my Park Avenue Baptist Church fam, Rev. Dr. Anna Carter-Florence, Dr. Cheryl Anderson, Candice Czubernat, Shae Washington, Jen Hatmaker, Uncle Danny and Auntie Abby, Evelyn of the Internets, Deborah Jian Lee, Kenji Kuramitsu, Jeff Chu, James Barnett, Satchell Drakes, Jonah Venegas, Hannah Paasch, Donald Scherschilt, Jenilee Dowling, Alicia Crosby, Bailey Wayne Hundl, Darin McKenna, Kaitlin Curtice, Tori Glass, Jett Johnson, Austin Hartke, Dr. Robyn Henderson-Espinoza, Isaac Archuleta, SueAnn Shiah, Lauren Wilde, Brit Barron, Brenda Marie Davies, Andre Henry, Treah Caldwell, Audrey Velez, George Mekhail, Hillary McBride, Micky ScottBey Jones, Mo, Audrey Assad, Antonia Terrazas, William Matthews, Diana Butler Bass, Sam Lamott, Rachel Francis, Anna Vos, Elliot Vos, Stefie Dominguez, Jared Byas, Corey Copeland, Micah J. Murray, Mellissa B. Hawks, AnaYelsi Velasco-Sanchez, Blaire Bohlen Rachael Ward, Matthew Paul Turner, Min. leea allen, Brené Brown, Elizabeth Gilbert, Mary Magdalene, St. Thomas, my brothers– Patrick, Robert, and Ryan, my cousins and extended fam, all the rest of my chosen fam, Lin Manuel-Miranda, Stacy Abrams, Maxine Waters, the entire cast of the NPR Politics Podcast, Tobin Low, Kathy Tu, Chani Nicholas, Kid Fury, Crissle, Lizzo, and Beyoncé.

I thank you, Spirit. You are the love that sustains me and in you I have perfect peace. Thank you for leading me out into the wilderness to find my freedom.

Finally, I want to thank my Body. You have loved me so well. You have protected me. You have helped me heal in ways I never knew possible. You are so exquisitely designed and I am in awe of your connection to Love. Keep me in it. Don't let me go. (I know you won't.) I love you. Let's do this more.

And finally, thank you, dear reader. I'm honored that you'd take time out of your life to read my words. I pray they bless you in whatever way is necessary to get you closer to Love.

Remember to take your meds, go see your therapist, drink some water, eat something delicious, move your body in a way that feels good, take a nap when you need to, cry more often without apology, and tell someone about this book because, bitch, I got bills to pay... lol. But for real, thanks for reading. Means a ton. See you on the internet, beloved.

ABOUT THE AUTHOR

Kevin Garcia (they/them) is a digital pastor, mystical theologian, spiritual teacher, and intuitive life coach based in Atlanta, GA. Their work focuses on creating spaces for people to find healing from spiritual trauma. As a creator, Kevin makes videos, writes publications, and hosts the podcast *A Tiny Revolution,* they seek to show people the power of ordinary people living revolutionary lives. They travel across the country to speak about queer identity, faith, intersectional justice, and the power of Love to heal ourselves and the world.

Additionally, Kevin is the creator of *Big Queer Adventure Co.,* a group dedicated to creating spaces and events for queer people to engage in spiritual healing, find chosen family, and rediscover their one wild life.

Kevin holds a Master of Arts in Practical Theology from Columbia Theological Seminary (May 2020) with an emphasis in preaching, worship, and the arts, as well as a Bachelor of Music in Vocal Music Education from Christopher Newport University.

To learn more about their work, their coaching, and their advocacy work, go to theKevinGarcia.com.

...

Bad Theology Kills was edited by Kit Kennedy of *Unchurchable: the podcast.*
The cover design was created by Kelsey Avera.
The headshot on is by Caleb Daniel, @ShotbyCXD in Atlanta, GA.

Made in the USA
Monee, IL
08 June 2021

70612900R10113